The Men of
FOX
COMPANY

History and Recollections of Company F,
291st Infantry Regiment,
Seventy-Fifth Infantry Division

EDGAR "TED" COX
AND
SCOTT ADAMS

iUniverse, Inc.
Bloomington

The Men of Fox Company
History and Recollections of Company F, 291st Infantry Regiment, Seventy-Fifth Infantry Division

iUniverse books may be ordered through booksellers or by contacting:

iUniverse
1663 Liberty Drive
Bloomington, IN 47403
www.iuniverse.com
1-800-Authors (1-800-288-4677)

Because of the dynamic nature of the Internet, any web addresses or links contained in this book may have changed since publication and may no longer be valid. The views expressed in this work are solely those of the author and do not necessarily reflect the views of the publisher, and the publisher hereby disclaims any responsibility for them.

Any people depicted in stock imagery provided by Thinkstock are models, and such images are being used for illustrative purposes only.

Certain stock imagery © Thinkstock.

ISBN: 978-1-4759-2736-8 (sc)
ISBN: 978-1-4759-2737-5 (hc)
ISBN: 978-1-4759-2738-2 (e)

Library of Congress Control Number: 2012909140

Printed in the United States of America

iUniverse rev. date: 7/18/2012

"We were all subdued by the day's pounding and the loss of close comrades. The column was very quiet, each man lost in his own thoughts as we trudged back to an area near Grand Halleux. We had survived another day!"

S/Sgt Dick Debruyn, Battle of the Bulge

CONTENTS

✶ ✶ ✶

INTRODUCTION

✳ ✳ ✳

THIS HISTORY OF Fox Company started in 2010, when Ted Cox sent Scott Adams a package of stories written by Fox Company veterans. Scott wanted to learn more about Fox Company. Scott had not pressed his father about World War II and Earl Adams like most men did not like to tell war stories. After talking to several children of Fox veterans, Scott was often told their fathers would rather tell humorous stories. For example, Earl Adams would tell the story of having some boar hogs chase his squad up trees. The squad stayed treed till they realized they had M1 rifles and the boar hogs did not.

By 2010 there were only eighteen Fox Company men still alive and several were not in good health. In Ted's package, there were accounts written by Sam Drake, Jack Reese, Dick Forni, Bill Hayes and Nathan Henn. There was a copy of Company G's newsletter, The Guidon, that included a long account of the Battle of the Bulge written by Dick Debruyn of Fox and a short piece by Sam Drake on Fox's march from Poteau. Ted had included several of the newsletters he had prepared over years, which included pieces of history from the War. Ted also included his written memories of the war. So this project was built upon memories of Fox written years earlier.

Several men reviewed the first draft of this book. Ray Stoddard provided his written memories and pictures. Ray also submitted a copy of Sam Drake's account of the attack from Grand Halleux and Fred Reither's memories of Fox Company, especially of the Louisiana Maneuvers. John Fetrow provided his input and mailed Scott copies of the newspapers the *Mule* and *Stars and Stripes* and the magazine *Yank*. Fetrow also provided photos. Ed Neville provided photos of the weapons platoon. Dick Siakel, Bob Stegen, Bob Berkebile and Dick Phillips provided their memories of the War. Richard Krosin, Grandson of Nathan Henn, provided copies of interviews he made with several Fox men for a college paper about the Battle of the Bulge. Ed Letourneau in 2000, was interviewed by a local TV Station where he told his memories of the war. Ed's daughter Leslie let Scott borrow the video. Geoff Arend provided photos collected by his father Hank Arend.

Genoa Stanford of the Fort Benning, Georgia Donovan Library supported the writing of this history by copying parts of the monthly 291st Infantry Regiment Actions against the enemy reports. The reports were on 70 year old micro film and hard to copy. These monthly reports show the development of the Regiment as a unit that could function in combat. All Infantry Regiments in World War II were to write monthly reports summarizing their actions in combat. The Donovan Library has these reports. The 291st Infantry Regiment did not write the monthly report for December until the first week in February 1945 and the report is short. The report for January was written the first week in February and is more detailed than December 1945. The reports for February and March were both written in the first week of the next month and the reports includes S3 operations overlays. The report for April is shorter reflecting that the operations were fast changing. The report ends with the 291st Infantry Regiment on the banks of the Ruhr River, where the Regiment changed over to military government duties.

This history uses, as general situation material, the pamphlet, *The 75th Infantry Division in Combat* written by the Division G3 section, the *Combat diary of the 291st Infantry Regiment, the History of the 291st Infantry Regiment April 15 1943 to Sept 1944*, the *291st Infantry Regiment action against the enemy reports for December 1944 to April 1945*.

Ted Cox had compiled a list of men who were killed and wounded. That list and an early 1980 address list that Ted used to organize reunions were the basis of the attempt to list the members of Fox Company. The list is long and everyone who reviewed it provided ranks of men, changes to spellings of names and information on what men did after the war. Fox Company started the war with 6 officers and 190 men. Fox went down to 2 officers and 65 men after the Bulge and Colmar. Then in Holland was brought back up to strength of 6 officers and 190 men. There were probably more than 400 men who served in Fox Company from its formation at Fort Leonard Wood, Missouri to its breakup at Camp Baltimore, France. In 2011, 303 men could be listed.

The Men of Fox Company

The men who served in Fox Company knew what they did in the war. This history is written so that their descendants will know their stories. This book attempts to give a feel of what the men of Fox Company endured during battle. Often the same battle is viewed by different members of Fox Company from company, platoon and squad level.

Edgar (Ted) Cox and Scott Adams

FORMATION AND TRAINING FOR WAR
✷ ✷ ✷

*Fox Company was the only company in the division to have
two squads in first place in individual proficiency tests*

THE 75TH INFANTRY DIVISION (ID) was called the "Diaper Division". It
was said the 75th ID had the youngest age of all Divisions committed to
Europe, because it had the average age, 21.9 years.[1] Stephen Ambrose,
in his book <u>D-Day</u> stated the average age of an American division was
twenty-six.[2] The 75th ID was thrown into combat soon after arriving in
Europe in December 1944. Over the next 94 days, the 75th ID fought
three campaigns. These were the Ardennes (Known as the Battle of
the Bulge), the Rhineland (Colmar Pocket) and Central Europe (Ruhr
Valley). Quickly the men of the 75th ID became seasoned combat
troops. For their efforts in stopping the western attack of the German
army in the Battle of the Bulge and the Colmar Pocket, the 75th ID was
known as the Bulge Busters. This history will follow Company F, 291st
Infantry Regiment, 75th ID through its battles. Each battle will be told
by several men from different levels of command to get different points
of view. During World War 2, the military phonetic alphabet used Fox
for the letter F. Therefore the men thought of their company as Fox
Company.

Fox Company was part of 2nd Battalion 291st Infantry Regiment of
the 75th ID. 2nd Battalion also included E, G, and H Companies. The
291st Infantry Regiment and the 75TH ID were formally activated at Fort
Leonard Wood, Missouri on April 15th 1943. Fort Leonard Wood was a
new post, built in 6 months in 1940 by a construction group that went

around the country building army bases.[3] The officer cadre had attended new officer training at Fort Benning, Georgia prior to their arrival at Fort Leonard Wood. The sergeant cadre came from the 83rd Infantry Division. But in Fox Company the cadre did not fill positions below platoon sergeant. The 291st Infantry Regiment had been organizing at Fort Leonard Wood since March 10th, 1943. Colonel Julian Dayton was the first regimental commander. At activation Major John Keenon was the first 2nd Battalion commander. Captain Gene Droulliard was the first Fox Company commander but soon was transferred to Company G as its commander. But not before naming several of the new enlisted men to be corporals. Captain James (Sam) Drake took command of the Fox and led it through State side training and took the company to war.

On April 19th 1943 mobilization training started. The majority of the young teenage soldiers came from reception centers without training. The training at Fort Leonard Wood included weapons training, bayonet and grenade instruction, patrolling, map reading, field fortifications. Training progressed from individual soldier to squad then platoon and finally company. Mobilization training was concluded on July 24, 1943. Battalion and regiment training came next, often spending weeks at a time on bivouac to adjust to field conditions. Many soldiers who started training in April were made sergeants. Athletic teams were formed. In the summer of 1943 many soldiers were able to go home on leave. Some soldiers were selected for deployment overseas. New trainees came from the Army Specialized Training Program (ASTP) to fill the gaps. The ASTP was a military training program allowing enlisted men to stay in college so that later the Army would have a source of junior officers or soldiers with technical skills.[4] One ATSP soldier was future Senator from Kansas, Bob Dole. Dole went through the Louisiana maneuvers training with the 290th regiment until the summer of 1944 when he went Infantry Officer Candidate School at Fort Benning, GA. Bob Dole went on to serve in the 10th Mountain Division in Italy[5] and later became a United States Senator from Kansas.

2nd Battalion command was passed to Lieutenant Colonel (LTC) Jesse Drain Jr., West Point Class of 1936. LTC Drain had been a War Department observer of the war in Italy prior to coming to Fort Leonard Wood. From 1952 to 1953, Jesse Drain was a Colonel and commanded the 7th Infantry Regiment in the Korean War.[6]

Photo by John Fetrow
Tents lined up for inspection of field gear at Fort Leonard Wood

PFC John Fetrow in his cook's whites at Fort Leonard Wood

Fort Leonard Wood: T/Sgt Dobbins, S/Sgt Adams, S/Sgt Goodyear, S/Sgt Berkebile, PFC John Fetrow. Adams, Goodyear & Berkebile were 2nd Platoon Squad leaders. Before shipping overseas, Dobbins was transferred out of Fox. Fetrow was in 1st squad 2nd platoon before going to cook's helper school.

Fort Leonard Wood 2nd Platoon with M1 rifles, caliber 30-06 (7.62mm), semi-automatic with an 8 round clip. Each 12 man squad was made up of 3 teams. Team Able was 2 scouts. Team Baker and Charlie were rifle teams. They moved by bounds with each team taking turns maneuvering and supporting by fire. There were 3 squads per rifle platoon and 3 rifle platoons per Company. The Company also had weapons platoon with 2 light machine guns and 2 60mm Mortars to support the rifle platoons and squads.

Adams with the Browning Automatic Rifle (BAR), Caliber 30-06 (7.62 mm) and had a 20 round magazine.

Each American Infantry squad had one BAR for fire support for its teams. The German squad had a light machine gun (MG34 or MG42) in its 10 man squad. German squad tactics were built around its machine gun. The German rifleman had a bolt action Mauser rifle.[7]

Fox's company basketball team won the Regimental Championship and the Divisional Championship. Team consisted of Ed Baronian, George Thomas, Del Goodyear, Carlos Chavez, LT William Murphy (coach), John Porter, James Cardoza, Cecil Helphinstine (team captain), Earl Adams, and Royal Elf.

In January 1944 the 75th ID left Fort Leonard Wood for the 6th Louisiana Maneuver Period. Training in Louisiana lasted from February through April 1944. The 75th ID along with the 92nd ID was part of XVIII Corps called the Blue force. The Blue force maneuvered, defended and attacked the Red Force consisting of the 44th ID and the 8th Armored Division. The maneuvers took place around Merryville, DeRider, and Camp Polk, Louisiana.[8] PFC Fred Reither remembers marching miles most days to set up road blocks and guarding bridges. After marching for miles many men including Reither had blisters for the medics to fix. On another march the company marched through a swamp and knee deep mud. They then crossed a river in assault boats to attack the enemy.

At the beginning of April 1944 the 75th ID was sent to Camp Breckinridge, Kentucky. At Camp Breckinridge individual training continued. Monetary awards were given to men who scored the highest totals in rifle marksmanship. During July and August the regiment was kept busy with squad and platoon proficiency tests, regimental combat team exercises and battalion combat firing tests. In a letter to his Aunt and Uncle in July, S/Sgt Earl Adams wrote that in squad tests S/Sgt George Thomas set the division record on one squad test and Adams got the record high on another squad test. Fox Company was the only company in the Division to have 2 squads in first place in individual proficiency tests . Adams wrote the "Old Man" (Capt Drake) was quite happy and it was good to have him on the good side.[9] Overnight bivouacs were common with several days spent in the field. From every theater of the war overseas veterans arrived along with soldiers from the infantry replacement training centers. When it was shown more infantrymen were needed, men were transferred to the Infantry. Some such as Ed Letourneau and Ed Neville came from Colleges and the ASTP. Men such as Ray Stoddard came from the Army Air Corps. Others such as Dick Forni, came from military police units.

Ed Letourneau joined Fox Company and 3rd platoon during the last part of the Louisiana Maneuvers. Ed had been in the ASTP program studying Engineering for 5 months at the City College of New York. Since the Army needed more soldiers for combat replacements, the ASTP was ended. Ed had taken Infantry basic before going to CCNY so he assigned to the 75th ID, while it was taking part in the Louisiana Maneuvers. At Camp Breckinridge, Ed became friends with John Klimek from Chicago. John wanted to get married before shipping out for Europe. John asked Ed to be his best man. John's family was Polish and John's father owned a tavern. The wedding celebrations lasted 3 days. During the Battle of the Bulge John Klimek was killed.

Ed Neville was also in the ASTP and joined Fox's mortar section of the weapons platoon at Camp Breckinridge. In Fox Company, Ed made friends with Cecil Brooks, William Evans, Arthur Giustizia, Gerald Dickinson and Ben Combs. Brooks, Evans, and Giustizia were killed in action. Ben Combs was wounded. Ed was hospitalized in January for several weeks with dysentery and trench foot. Ed and Ben stayed friends after the war. After the war Ed married Marjorie Thon. His first date with Marjorie was with Ben and his wife Anne.

The Company posed for photos for 75th Infantry Division book produced by Albert Love Enterprises.[10]

Company photographs taken at Camp Breckinridge, KY Headquarters and 1st Platoon, Front row 3rd from left LT. Hanser, 4th LT Thompson, 5th Capt. Sam Drake, 6th LT. Bowman, 7th 1st Sgt Sigmund. Top row 1st on right , Cpl Ray Stoddard, 2nd row, 1st on right, PFC Jerry Goldman.

2nd Platoon and headquarters men

3rd platoon and weapons platoon

In the early summer 1944 members of Fox Company took the Expert Infantryman Badge (EIB) test. This was a field craft and weapons skill test that only a few pass. To compete, you had to first qualify as an expert marksman with the M1 Rifle. By orders dated July 15, 1944, eleven men from Fox Company were awarded the EIB. They were the following: S/Sgt Rupert Buchanan, S/Sgt Ernest Porter, S/Sgt Orville Reagan, S/Sgt George Thomas, T/Sgt Oris Dobbins, T/Sgt Cecil Helphinstine, Sgt Thomas Cardoza, Sgt Gordon Harvey, Sgt Merle Johnson, Cpl Cecil Brooks, and PFC Richard DeBruyn.

For one Battalion exercise, Captain Drake assigned Corporal Ray Stoddard the mission of conducting one of the training stations. Ray was to lead training in compass reading, which Ray protested that he knew nothing about compass readings. Drake gave Ray a soldier's manual and told him to study it. But Drake took it upon himself to ensure Ray was ready to teach the subject. Drake led he did not push.

At Camp Breckinridge, Lieutenant (LT) Ted Cox arrived to be Capt Sam Drake's company executive officer. Platoon leaders were Richard Thompson (1st Platoon), Harvey P. Cannon (2nd Platoon), William (Bill) Hanser (3rd Platoon), and Paul K (PK) Bowman (Weapons Platoon).

First Sergeant was 1Sgt David Sigmund.

Tech Sergeant (T/Sgt) George Thomas was the 1st Platoon Sergeant. S/Sgt Orville Reagan was platoon guide. After the Battle of the Bulge, the 1st Platoon squad leaders were S/Sgt Richard (Dick) DeBruyn, S/Sgt Chuck Pippy, S/Sgt Elmer Prestridge.

2nd Platoon Sergeant was T/Sgt "Pappy" French. Platoon guide S/Sgt Pearson Schiller. 2nd Platoon squad leaders were S/Sgt Robert T.

Berkebile (1ˢᵗ Squad), and S/Sgt Del Goodyear (2ⁿᵈ Squad), S/Sgt Earl R Adams (3ʳᵈ Squad).

3ʳᵈ Platoon Sergeant T/Sgt Irwin, S/Sgt Clarence Shelton was platoon guide. 3ʳᵈ platoon squad leaders were S/Sgt Merle Johnson, S/Sgt Donnie Glasscock, and S/Sgt Shea.

Weapons Platoon Sergeant T/Sgt George Thompson and T/Sgt Lee Albers, S/Sgt Earnest Porter, Mortar Section Sergeant, S/Sgt Ed Neville Neville, mortar squad leader.

Sports took their place in the Regimental activities. Soldiers formed boxing, baseball and basketball teams. The Fox Company basketball team won the Regimental and Divisional championship again with Captain Sam Drake as coach. Earl Adams wrote home from Camp Breckinridge that in the two seasons Fox's basketball team lost one game.

To keep soldiers informed about items of interest and recreational activities, a regimental newspaper was published. The newspaper was called the *Rigamarole*. The 75ᵗʰ Division printed a newspaper called *The Mule.*

Nathan Henn at Camp Breckenridge in front of Library, Summer 1944

As stated at the beginning of this story, the 75ᵗʰ ID had the youngest average age of its soldiers. For example the squad leader of 3ʳᵈ squad 2ⁿᵈ platoon, Earl Adams, turned 21 in October 1944. His squad scout, Dick Phillips, was eighteen in October 1944. At the time of deployment to

Europe, the Army regulations stated an eighteen years old soldier did not have to serve overseas. Captain Drake told Dick Phillips he did not have to deploy. But Dick did not want to go to war with any other unit, so he deployed and turned nineteen in England.[11]

Before the 75th ID shipped out, some families were able to visit. Viola Edge came to see her husband PFC Kay Edge. PFC James Davis's wife and 3 oldest children came to say goodbye. His oldest son, Bill was only 4 and a half but he remembers Camp Breckinridge. He also remembers Viola Edge was very kind to his mother and the children. S/Sgt Earl Adams' mother travelled to Kentucky.

At midnight with bands playing on October 16, 1944, Fox Company and the 75th ID moved by train to Camp Shanks, New York, arriving October 18 in the afternoon. Dubbed "Last Stop USA," the Camp Shanks housed about 50,000 troops spread over 2,040 acres and was the largest World War II Army embarkation camp.

GOING OVER SEAS

✷ ✷ ✷

*If there had not been the mistake in routing troop trains,
it would have been the 75th Infantry Division at the point
of the German attack in the Battle of the Bulge*

ON OCTOBER 21ᵀᴴ THE 291ˢᵗ Infantry Regiment boarded the U.S. Army Transport, the SS Edmund B Alexander and steamed out of New York harbor past the Statue of Liberty on October 22nd. SS Alexander joined a large convoy and arrived at Swansea, South Wales on November 2nd. There were several German U boat scares. Sub chasers and destroyers sped around once in a while and dropped depth chargers. According to reports one submarine was sunk. Fred Reither remembers for the first few days blimps flew overhead. Besides troop ships the convoy include aircraft carriers, cruisers and destroyers. The weather on the crossing was good. There was not much to do on the crossings. There were life boat drills to train the soldiers where to go to man a life boat. The Alexander was a converted passenger liner. Ed Letourneau remembers the bunks were three high and many soldiers were sea sick.

The officers had it better than the enlisted men. Officers had private quarters and ate in the ship's officer dining hall with white table clothes and Filipino waiters. After dinner, card games would be played. LT Ted Cox won $400 by the time the ship reached Wales, which he sent home to his wife and young son.

November 2nd the ship arrived at Swansea. The troops left the ship at dark and took a train ride to Haverfordwest, Wales. By truck they went to Camp Picton. It was cold. The 291ˢᵗ spent about 30 days in South

Wales, organizing equipment, physical conditioning, marching with field equipment and unit drills. Ted Cox remembers "We were under blackout conditions and did not know it, until a uniformed Bobbie knocked on our door after dark and informed us to put curtains on our windows."

On December 9, 1944 Fox Company left Haverfordwest at 11pm and took a train ride to South Hampton arriving at 8am. Fox boarded a British ship, the SS Empire Javelin, at South Hampton and crossed the channel to Le Havre, France. Ted Cox recalls, "The ship was small and the seas rough. The officers ate with the ship's officers in their mess. The food was good but the quantity was small. At 9 o'clock in the morning and 3 o'clock in the afternoon, everything stopped while the British had their tea. Of course we were invited and we accepted because our stomachs were empty because of the small amount of food we had. With the tea we were served one small cookie and there were no seconds. We learned that they were short on food so they had to get by with a smaller amount. We Americans were accustomed to eating all we wanted. The crossing was rough and many were sea sick." Fred Reither remembers the trip was crowded and had bad food. The troops played cards. On December 11, the SS Empire Javelin arrived at Le Havre and the men and equipment are barged to shore. Troops had to go down cargo nets to get into landing craft. On line you can read <u>The Battle Diary of Jack Graber and Company I-291st Infantry, 75th Division</u>. Jack wrote the he sailed to France on the SS Empire Javelin. The SS Empire Javelin was built in the United States and given to the British under the Lend Lease Act. was not without danger. On December 23, 1944 less than a month after the 75th ID crossed the English Channel, two Infantry Regiments of the 66th ID boarded the SS Leopoldville to cross the English Channel. Five and one half miles off Cherbourg, France, the SS Leoleopoldville was struck by a torpedo from a German U Boat. The ship sank slowly and over 1400 soldiers were saved. But 763 soldiers were killed, many were key leaders.[12] It took time to reconstitute the 66th, so they were used to contain German units trapped in pockets along the coast of France. Then on December 28, 1944, the SS Empire Javelin that had carried the 291st Regiment to France was sunk. It is not known if it was sunk by a U boat or by a mine. Nearby ships got all of the 1400 troops and most of the sailors off the stricken ship. Only a few sailors near the explosion died.[13]

From Le Havre the company boarded trucks and drove under black out conditions about 50 miles northeast of Le Harve. Fox Company set up a bivouac near Saint Paer, France.

Left to Right Capt Drake, LT Cox, LT Cannon, LT Bowman after arriving in France. Soon during the Battle of the Bulge, LT Bowman would be killed and Capt Drake seriously wounded. LT Cox would take command of Company F and LT Cannon would take command of Company E.

Ted Cox saved a newspaper clipping of Edward Wolf's letter to the Editor. Wolf was acting as assistant transportation officer for the 75th ID, when it was to be moved by train to the port of embarkation. The Infantry Regiments had moved by train to Camp Shanks, NY. But the troop trains did not go back to Camp Breckinridge to get the rest of the Division. Instead the trains were sent to Camp McCoy, WI, where the 106th ID was stationed. A decision was made to load the trains with the men and equipment of the 106th ID. Therefore the 106th ID was shipped to Europe before the 75th ID.[14] The 106th ID was sent to the front lines in the Ardennes, which was supposed to be a quiet area. Instead they were at the point of the German's attack for the start of the Battle of the Bulge. Two Infantry Regiments were surrounded and were forced to surrender. Only one Infantry Regiment, the 424th Infantry Regiment, and Division Artillery were able to escape the German attack. If there had not been the mistake in routing troop trains, it would have been the 75th ID at the point of the German attack for the Battle of the Bulge. If there had not been the mistake the 75th ID would have been on the front lines being attacked by five Armored Divisions and twelve Infantry Divisions. Instead of the 106th ID, it would have been units of the 75ID being destroyed or captured. Combat veterans often say luck played a large part in surviving combat.

BATTLE OF THE BULGE

★ ★ ★

The temperature was twenty degrees below zero, with two feet of snow. The soldiers slept in the woods, usually three men would put their shelter halves together and sleep close together to keep warm.

THE 75TH DIVISION WAS to go and join the 9th Army about 300 miles away. Instead because of the German Army attack in the Ardennes, the company moved on December 20th by truck about 250 miles to Tongeren, Belgium. The 75th ID was assigned to the 7th Corps, 1st Army on the north side of the Bulge that the Germans had made. The German plan was to attack and seize the Port of Antwerp, Belgium, a major port the allies were using to supply the allied armies on the northern flank. At this time, the German Army held the Netherlands (Holland). Hitler's plan by seizing Antwerp and linking up with his forces in the Netherlands would cut off the British 21st Army Group, under General Montgomery, and the US 1st and 9th Army. His future plan was to destroy the cut off British and US armies. Hitler then planned that the German Army would attack the allied force in France. He hoped victories on the battlefield would allow Germany to negotiate a peace treaty with the British and Americans. Hitler would then be able to concentrate on fighting the Russians. German Generals thought the plan was too ambiguous but could not change Hitler's decisions. In the end the German Generals were correct, the plan was meant to fail.[15]

From December 21st to the 27th the Division Headquarters, Division support units and 291st were in reserve. The 289th and 290th Infantry Regiments were attached to 3rd Armored Division. On December 24th, 2nd

Battalion, 291st Infantry Regiment was attached to Combat Command A, 2nd Armored Division vicinity of Rochefort. The 2nd Armored men were rough and tough men that had been in many fire fights. To the Fox men, these were real veterans. Fred Reither remembers defensive positions outside city of Marche. While attached to 2nd Armored, Fox learned of the Malmedy massacre, where captured American soldiers were lined up and shot. In no uncertain terms, the Armored Battalion commander told Fox Company were we not to take prisoners. Someone asked what to do with them. He was dead serious when he said we were to do what the Germans did. Then he said the best thing to do was not let anyone surrender.

Fox Company rode on tanks to road blocks and patrolled in front of the tank positions. The book "A Combat diary of the 291st Infantry Regiment" reported Company F and E rode tanks on December 26th and attacked enemy outpost near Rochefort, Belgium. Fox men would ride on tanks until they took hostile fire and then they would dismount and return fire. With the firepower Fox had with their M1 Garand semiautomatic rifles and the tanks with their 76 mm cannon and machine guns, the Germans would soon be overwhelmed. Then they would move on to their next target. 2nd Battalion made its first battalion attack on the night of December 27th on the enemy at Rochefort. Despite the fact the battalion had to withdraw later that evening, a creditable job was done under their first Baptism of fire. The actions of 2nd Armored Division and 2nd Battalion helped stop the western movement of the attack by the Germans. They kept the Germans from crossing the Meuse River and from going on to the Capital Brussels. Without the crossing of the Meuse, the German objective of capturing Antwerp was lost. Also by keeping the Germans from crossing the Meuse, the Germans were unable to capture the large Allied supply base of fuel and ammunition west of Liege. Without fuel the German attack would fail. Irwin Chitwood recalls passing a line of German tanks and other vehicles at Grandmenil. The vehicles were not destroyed in combat but had run out of fuel.

Before going on the offensive Fox set up road blocks. The Germans never tried to attack the road blocks. It is assumed the Germans were waiting to gather enough force to over run the road blocks. In a letter dated January 8, 1945, S/Sgt Earl Adams wrote home that he and his squad had manned a road block. The German came close enough to hear their voices and he could hear their tanks moving around. But the

Germans did not try to force their way through Adams's road block. Early the next morning Fox and 2nd Armored surprised the Germans with their own attack.

After heavy fighting, Fox and 2nd Armored stopped the German drive. After retaking the town of Houffalize on the 28th and 29th of December, Fox and 2nd Armored went their separate ways. Along with the 2nd Armored Division, 2nd Battalion was cited in the Order of the Day of the Belgian Army for action in the Ardennes. 2nd Battalion was awarded the Belgian Croix De Guerre by orders dated April 28, 1947.

Fox had trained hard for combat. Some men had been training for war since April 1943. Fox was considered green because they lacked combat. That soon would change but it was not easy turning into a combat veteran. Dick Phillips remembers the straight rows of trees in the Ardennes. Dick was watching down a row when a German soldier stepped out of the row of trees. Without thinking Phillips pulled the trigger, killing for the first time. He moved back behind the trees and then got sick.

On December 27th, 2nd Battalion had the first casualties of the 291st Regiment. Pvt Albert Main and Pvt Raymond Gardner of H Company were killed.

Around December 28th, the 2nd Battalion rejoined the 291st Infantry Regiment and moved to Villers Sainte Getrude. 2nd battalion was in reserve. Everyone was nervous because of reports that Germans had infiltrated behind our lines wearing American uniforms. The company issued passwords and counter signs but often men would forget so the men asked questions like which baseball team played in Brooklyn. Fred Reither remembers marching through the cold to a defensive position overlooking the town of Gran Manile. He remembers plenty of artillery, tank battles and infantry skirmishes. He slept in a foxhole with PFC Francis Quinn. After January 1, 1945 the company marched through the ruins of Gran Manile into a new wooded area. Reither remembers moving by truck to Spa, Belgium, where they got good food and were billeted in houses. Around January 9th, Fox marched from Spa in high snow. Reither had dysentery and had to fall out and spent several days in a tent hospital near Spa,

LT Cox and a sergeant were given a task from higher ups to measure craters created by German artillery. They measured how far the dirt was thrown and take a compass reading to determine the direction the shell came from. The idea was that by plotting the lines from different craters and seeing where the lines intersected, you could determine the location of German artillery. Who ever got the data was never able to shut up the German artillery.

On Christmas day the weather cleared and flights of B-17's flew over at about 10,000 to 20,000 feet. One flight of 18 was overhead when German anti-aircraft weapons (probably 88's) opened up and about 9 bombers were hit. Some airmen were able to parachute from their bombers. One bomber exploded and no one got out. While patrolling tin foil was found hanging on the trees. At first it was thought it was a way to help the GI's celebrate Christmas but later it was learned the tin foil was dropped by bombers to cause the German radar to malfunction.

The weather was about 20 degrees below zero and with two feet of snow. The soldiers slept in the woods, usually 3 men would put together their tent halves and sleep close together to stay warm.

While in reserve, LTC Drain ordered Fox Company to take a machine gun section to assist 3rd Battalion in repelling a German attack. Drain said the machine gun section should go overland because the highway was under German control. Capt. Drake sent LT Cox on the mission with two light machine guns, two jeeps with trailers and 8 men. They followed an old road through the woods when they came under small arms fire. Before they could ascertain where the fire was coming from it stopped. They never knew who or where the firing was from. They traveled about a mile when they came to a steep hill. The highway was about 300 yards west of them and there was a patch of woods at the bottom of the hill. The road led them up the hill and just as they almost reached the top, the ice was so slick all jeeps could do was spin and spin. They unhooked the trailers and with all men pushing they could not get one jeep over the top of the hill. It was almost 4 o'clock in the afternoon. LT Cox had the men wait in the woods while he set out on foot to find their objective. LT Cox walked about a mile or two but found nothing. He could not hear any weapons firing, as if a major battle was going on. In this area like a lot of Europe the forest was thickly planted in rows, like a tree farm. There were rows of trees with fire lanes between. As LT Cox walked his way back to his men, he saw to the west down a fire lane a GI truck about 200 yards away. Walking towards the truck he saw the driver with his rifle pointed at him. LT Cox knew that there had been reports of Germans wearing American uniforms behind the line. When LT Cox got within 20 feet of the driver, he was ordered to stop. LT Cox convinced the driver he was a friendly and was lost. It turned out the driver was also lost. LT Cox and the truck driver drove up and down fire lanes and old roads looking for 3rd Battalion for about an hour with no luck. It was getting dark so LT Cox dismissed the driver so he could find his own unit. LT Cox walked back to the patch of woods and found his men. They spent the night in the woods. The next day LT. Cox took two men and set out walking to find their objective. Sure enough, after about a mile further than they had previously gone, they found 3rd Battalion. Brigadier General (BG) Mickle the assistant division commander was there. LT Cox told them about the problems with icy hills. BG Mickel asked why they did not use the highway as he had just driven over it. LT Cox said "this is today and that was yesterday". The general must have been satisfied since he did not chew LT Cox out. As it turned out it was a wild goose chase. The battle was over yesterday, the day they had orders to assist them. LT Cox went back to the bivouac area, gathered up the men and jeeps, found the highway and went back to join the company.

From December 30th to December 31st the entire Regiment occupied defensive positions in the vicinity of the following Belgian towns, Chene-al-Pierre, Vaux-Chavanne and Manhay. The mission was to block German movement through Manhay to Liege.

Because of the dense woods, trucks and trailers were left on the fire lanes. Fox Company's trailer was in the fire lane when a major told Mess Sergeant Donald Nadeau to move the trailer to the edge of the woods because troops were to be moving through the area. The company two and a half ton truck had been sent on another mission, so the trailer could not be moved. The major came by again and ordered Don to move the trailer. Don flagged down a passing truck so the trailer was moved. When Don came back the next morning to retrieve the trailer it was gone and never found. It was lesson learned that GI's would steal from other GI's. Luckily Don had unloaded the stoves and most of the cooking equipment that was in the trailer and the two and a half ton truck, so his team was able to cook. Later Fox Company got another trailer. When equipment was lost, the Army required a report of survey. This was an investigation to see if someone should have to pay for the lost equipment. This made sense in peace time. But when Don got another trailer, higher headquarters demanded a report of survey. Don said that Capt Sam Drake told the higher headquarters it was lost during war and Fox was not doing a report of survey.[16]

Don and his cooks, Cpl Andy Anderson, T/5 Charles Holt, Sgt George Grubbs, PFC John Fetrow and PFC Grover Hardy tried to feed Fox Company twice a day, in the morning before sunlight and in the evening after dark. Because the cooks were busy cooking early in the morning and worked at night, they were excluded from duties such as being on Command Post (CP) security or patrols. Sometimes a hot meal had to be discarded because the fighting kept the cooks from delivering the meal. The kitchen was often located close behind the front lines, within artillery range. Company records show PFC Grover Hardy was wounded on January 17, 1945.

Shows Fox Company mess trailer in action at Fort Leonard Wood

On New Years Eve at midnight every artillery piece in Belgium opened up and sent the Germans a New Years greeting.

The 75th ID relieved the 82nd Airborne Division starting on January 10th ,1944. Part of the 82nd had defended Grand Halleux. The following was written by Corporal (Cpl) Ray Stoddard. Cpl Stoddard served in the company headquarters as a radio man, company sniper and as a company runner (messenger). Cpl Stoddard was armed with a 1903 A3 Springfield 30 caliber rifle with a scope.

"We were reformed and marched all night long through deep snow and we were urged by our officers to hike at quick time. This push continued until the wee hours of morning when, dog-tired, we joined our shelter halves into tents and bivouacked in a grove of pine trees on ground covered with over a foot of snow. Then with only a couple hours rest we packed up, gulped a semi hot breakfast served in our mess kits and continued hiking to a little town (a few buildings). Even before settling in, I was given an assignment to man a forward observation post with orders to phone headquarters if I saw enemy movement. We had relieved other troops and this observation post had been wired by the signal corps. I can remember a whole entanglement of wires entering the OP and disappearing in the snow to the rear. The walls of this post had been packed with snow reminiscent of the snow forts we built as boys in Minnesota. It protruded out from a ledge high on a steep hill and looked out on a panorama of snow-covered valleys and low hills. Now imagine this scene that I viewed taking place in the valley. A battle was in progress, and I watched hypnotically from my box seat at the ant-sized figures moving across a field in an irregular line. All the while black splotches of shells were bursting in the snow in front of them. I could hear the muted sounds of gunfire and mortar fire and could see that in spite of all this heavy fire the troops in the valley, which I later learned were the boys of the 82nd Airborne Division, were pushing towards a dark forest. As darkness set in, the noise silenced and trailed off into quiet. I often imagined that if I were to compare what I saw that day it would be equal to scenes described in Tolstoy's War and Peace. Little did I anticipate that the next day (in very early predawn) we would be slogging down that very steep hill, gingerly crossing a frozen stream, the Salm River, and picking our way on rocks and logs."[17]

In the book *Hitler's Last Gamble*, LT Robert Justice of E Company 2nd Battalion, 291st Infantry Regiment was quoted concerning this long night's march to relieve the 82nd Airborne Division. LT Justice stated the march lasted eleven hours and covered 22 miles on icy roads with deep snow and the temperature was bitter cold.[18]

The 75th ID took part in the XVIII Airborne Corps coordinated attack to retake Saint Vith and its vital road net. Major General (MG) Ridgeway, the XVIII Airborne Corps Commander, ordered the 75th ID to attack south from across the Salm River to capture Vielsam, which was west of Saint Vith. The plan was for the 291st Infantry to attack and seize the ground north of the town and 289th Infantry was to attack and seize the high ground south of the town. This would make the whole valley untenable for the enemy, forcing the Germans to withdraw.

The 75th ID was ordered to attack the Germans and on January 14th our battalion was given orders to attack out of Grand Halleux. 291st Infantry Regiment would attack with 1st Battalion attacking on the right and 2nd Battalion on the left. 3rd Battalion was to support by fire. E & G companies of 2nd Battalion were to attack with Fox Company in reserve. The Fox CP was in a cellar of a house at one end of the town. As Executive Officer, Cox's job was to care of the CP, relay orders, see that ammunition was supplied and other things.

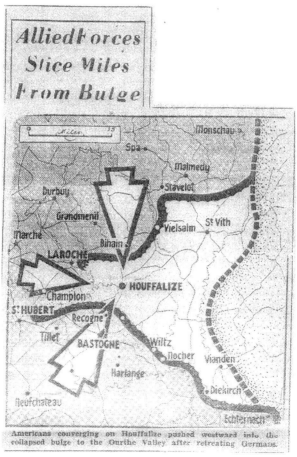

Stars and Stripes map from front page of January 14, 1944 issue.
The same issue stated the Russians had attacked into Poland.[19] Used with
permission from Stars and Stripes © 1945, 2012 Stars and Stripes.

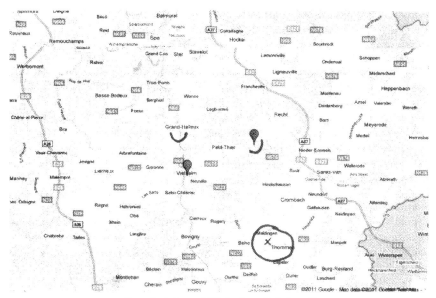

Google Map of Vielsalm, Belgium[20]

Map of area of operations for Fox Company in Belgium. In the center at the left balloon is Vielsam. 2nd Battalion attacked from Grand Halleux to the north of Vielsam. Fox was in reserve at Grand Halleux and marked with a black arc facing south. Next Fox Company went to defend at Poteau, at the right hand balloon and marked with a black arc facing southeast. The Germans were attacking from Saint Vith, to the southeast of Poteau. Fox Company's final battle in the Battle of the Bulge was at Aldringen. The location of Aldringen is marked with an X and surrounded by a black circle. Aldringen is due south from Poteau. Aldringen just a short distance south of the town of Maldingen.

After a 20 minute barrage on the woods outside of Grand Halleux, the attack began at 0730, January 15th. E & G were pinned down in a field after advancing 400 yards. Many of these men were killed and wounded by small arms fire and mortars. Every time one of them moved, the burp guns would open up. The Germans were dug in the edge of the woods and were bunkered in the ground with logs over the top and earth that withstood all the artillery that was thrown in. And there was a lot of it that landed right on top of them but never hurt them.

The following was written by Captain Sam Drake about the attack from Grand Halleux. Fox Company was holding a forward position just below Grand Halleux prior to the attack. We were to patrol and operate a forward observation post (OP) along the stream on the outskirts of town.

"Early on the morning of the attack we had built a crossing over the stream and moved into our position to support E and G in their attack. I did not see the attacking Companies take off. I had my men occupy a defiladed position between the line of departure (LOD) and Grand Halleux."

"As I remember, the attack was delayed one day. This probably gave the Germans a warning that an effort to dislodge them from the woods would be made. The Germans had good visibility of the field of action. My OP was along the fence line on the crest of the LOD. I recall a rifle bullet going through a small sapling just above my head. A Battalion officer was hit several times when he was right beside me. I dragged him into my slit trench and later crawled out with him and dragged him down into H Company area. I had blood all over me too. There he was evacuated."

"Watching the attack was one of the worst days of my life. After the attacking Companies were pinned down in that open, snow covered field, it was pitiful and heart searing feeling to watch the Germans shoot into any olive drab uniform that moved. I never felt so helpless in my life."

"The Battalion Command Post (CP) was in an area about 50 yards to the front of the slit trench that I had dug and on the forward slope of the attacking LOD and somewhat exposed.. The Battalion CP was under mortar and artillery fire. Their radio was out. I made several trips to the Battalion CP relaying messages from Lieutenant Colonel (LTC) Drain to Division Headquarters. He asked the Division Commanding officer for permission to pull back, reorganize and reform for another try. Their answer was a definite NO! I carried this message to him. The Battalion CP had been hit. I recall Captain Haddock of H Company lying there apparently dead. Later I heard that both his legs had been severed and that he recovered."

"Later I met BG Mickle, the Division second in command. He stated that at the time of my call, MG Ridgeway, the Corps CO was present and would not permit any pull back in any situation. The attack had been hopelessly stalled."

"I ran down to the Battalion CP and talked to LTC Drain, suggesting that I should bring up Fox Company and carry on the attack. However, it would be best to call in more artillery on the woods edge. I moved back to where my radio was located under a little cover. I talked to Division HQ about more artillery fire on the woods. A time was set and I had made plans to bring up the men. However the company had been moved back into a safer position. I could not contact them in time for the follow up of the artillery fire. I was not ordered by LTC Drain to move in and thought it would be useless to go in late."

"My radio and radio bearer were on the right part of the LOD. There was some cover but I'm sure it was visible to the enemy. I had two of my officers in a deep double foxhole behind me. While I was lying in the snow talking to Division, I recall looking up and could almost see a shell of some kind coming in. It may have been a mortar shell. It landed in that foxhole a few feet to my rear. After the explosion I yelled, "Anyone hurt?" LT Bowman of Weapons Platoon weekly said, "Me." That was his last word. The other officer had an injury. I think I was the target. I was fired on several times during my trips to the Battalion CP. In the foxhole where LT Bowman was, there was a frozen body of an 82nd Paratrooper. The Germans evidently had that area zeroed in."

"As you can see Fox Company did not move in to the attack. Later around dusk, the Company occupied the Line of Departure (LOD). We were strung out over the jump-off position of Companies E & G. We were ready for any enemy attack and hopefully could help survivors. Some worked their way back around dusk. It was hard to realize how anyone in the frozen, bloody field survived. It was 10 degrees below zero."

"After we moved up I remember hearing a wounded man cry for help. I asked for volunteers to go with me for a search. Many boys were lying out there in the field. All we saw, we touched and looked for signs of life. The only one I found alive was LT Petersen on G Company. As soon as I touched him and knew he was alive. I could not open Petersen's fingers. They were frozen. Petersen was then brought out and survived". Ironically LT Peterson died after the War in a jeep crash in France.

That day made me extremely bitter toward the Germans. We were rough on any we caught with anything American on their persons. That was one of the hardest days of my life. I was constantly on the move all day. I finally went back to my HQ in Grand Halleux, physically and mentally exhausted. That day will remain in my life forever!"[21]

During the day as this battle went on, LT Cox got curious as to what was going on where Capt. Drake was. He decided to go up to the front. As Cox made his way up the street of Grand Halleux, artillery shells kept coming in. He could hear them coming so would duck behind a big stone wall and the shells would land in the town not too far from me. Cox saw several men, who did not take cover when the shells would come in, get hit by shrapnel."

As Cox made his way up a hill in open ground on his way to the top where Drake was, mortar rounds kept falling near by. Every time one would hit he would hit the dirt or jump in a crater. Mortar rounds do not give a warning, they drop in unannounced. After you hear the explosion you knew you're still alive. There were some large chunks of shrapnel from them that would whirr through the air as Cox lay in a crater, but none hit him.

At the top of the hill in a clump of trees overlooking the battlefield where E & G companies were fighting, Cox found Capt. Drake, with LT Hanser, LT Bowman and several enlisted men. Capt Drake evidently had orders to commit Fox Company to the battlefield right through where E & G were pinned down".

LT Hanser had been given the assignment with his platoon, and he was arguing that it would be suicide to across the open ground. Capt Drake was talking to BG Mickel, assistant Division Commander, on the radio and Mickel was telling him that he would get artillery barrages to soften up the Germans.

Now it was easy to see that the artillery was doing no good as it had been pouring on the German position all day. Drake wanted to attack from a flank, but the General was insisting that he go across the open field.

We were occupying some 2 man foxholes at the time, or sitting on the sides of them to observe the action. Cox was with a sergeant. Hanser and Bowman were in one foxhole and Drake was lying in the snow talking on the radio. They heard a shell coming in. Hanser called out that Bowman was hit. Drake asked how bad and Hanser answered that it was pretty bad. Bowman became our first KIA. Quite a few men joined him later.

Anyway the attack was finally called off for the day, we went back to the CP. That night some men carried Bowman back down the hill so the burial detail could get him."

That night Capt Drake and others went out into the open field looking for any men that might be still be alive. Capt Drake found only Lt Peterson alive. Other men found some men alive and these guys can thank Drake and others for saving their lives, as they would have frozen to death that night. Lt Peterson was brought to Fox's CP. Cpl Mumford took care of his wounds. Drake came to the CP and found three men sleeping on the floor. Drake chewed them out. He had told them to be ready to go out with the stretcher and here they were sleeping. They got up in a hurry.

The next day 1st and 3rd Battalions attacked, but the Germans had pulled out during the night and they met little resistance. 2nd Battalion was placed as the Regimental reserve. A reinforced platoon from Fox was sent out as a combat patrol to a position on the left flank of the Regiment, to block suspected enemy operations and tie in with the left flank of the 3rd Battalion. The remainder of Fox was given the mission of sweeping the woods between the 3rd Battalion and the Division boundary.[22]

In 1995 Peter Dounis wrote in an article for the 75th veterans newsletter, the Bulge Busters, that Company G had 30 men killed, 33 wounded and 2 missing at Grand Halleux. A history of the 75th ID stated Company E had 13 killed at Grand Halleux.[23]

The 75th ID was not equipped with the proper gear for the cold weather. Jack Bell a reporter with the Minneapolis Star Journal and Chicago Daily News filed a report from the 75th ID on the poor clothing and resulting cold weather injuries. The article included a statement from a supply officer that red tape was slowing delivery of dry clothes. Field jackets were light weight and were standard olive drab. The Germans had white overcoats to blend in with the snow. Gloves issued were not designed for ten degrees below zero. The soldiers did not have proper boots. The so called boots were shoes with spats like tops. Leather boots would not be issued until March, just before the attack into Germany. Many soldiers suffered from trench foot and frozen feet and hands.[24]

It was hard coping with the cold and the snow. Bob Berkebile remembers how hard it was to sleep. "It was difficult to be in a deep sleep. You crawl into a foxhole or slit trench and try to keep warm and it is almost impossible. When you are cold it is impossible to get any deep sleep. You got what rest you could. And about the time you get to sleep somebody is nudging you saying, "Hey its your turn for guard duty."[25]

The following is Corporal Ray Stoddard's memory of the attack from Grand Halleux. "My attire consisted of a "tankers jacket" acquired earlier when we were with the 2nd Armored, OD woolen trousers and Army issue shoes. I had no gloves, having lost them quite a while before. I should have had a shelter half but I had tossed it a few days before when

I thought I was so fortunate to find an already dug foxhole. I bedded down in this deep hole, first laying the shelter half down, then wrapping my blanket around me and dropping off to sleep in that snowy hole. Upon awakening, I sniffed the air around me; it was like a sewer, a real stink!. That hole that I had so luckily found had been used as a toilet. My warm body had melted a big pile of shit lining the bottom. My shelter half was saturated with the melted crap. I was so damn mad at this nauseating stench that all I could do was fling the shelter half, but I kept my blanket and cleaned it as best I could in the snow."

"So we trudged down that hill that early AM, my soiled blanket rolled up and tied around my shoulders. A cotton bandoleer containing 1903 A3 Springfield 30 caliber cartridge clips was hung across my chest. My helmet liner had a spare pair of socks and a packet of toilet paper from a "K" ration tucked in the webbing. To complete my combat attire, I had a canteen, first aid pack and entrenching shovel attached to my cartridge belt. My scope equipped rifle was slung over my shoulder leaving my stiff gloveless hands free to tuck under my armpits. I figured the temperature was in the range of 10 below zero. The snow crunched under our shoes and our breath was misting and forming frost on the face. We silently trudged along, our thoughts to ourselves. We could be on a road but the snow and the darkness made it hard to tell. We came to a town, Grand Halleux, and passed a church. There seemed to be activity around the church but we kept going to a barnyard a little further along. While getting settled there Captain Drake called me and a comrade, an Italian boy from Brooklyn, Tom Milana, to be company runners (liaison) between regiment and him. So we hiked up a hill attached to a new group of guys. As I recall, LTC Drain was the leader. On reaching the top of the hill there was a lot of conversation and muddling around within this group (I guess they were giving orders as to how the jump off attack was going to go). It was just breaking light and Tom and I were standing there stamping our feet to keep the feeling in them when "ALL HELL BROKE LOOSE" mortar fire (maybe artillery fire) started landing around us and suddenly everybody scattered and vanished. Tom and I headed for a low ditch and began digging in but my shovel hit something below the snow. It was a long box held together by wires to a similar box. We had never seen anything like this but quickly assessed that this was tank mine. We quit digging and chopping and buried ourselves as deeply as possible in the snow on top of these mines. While we are coping with this we began hearing the rapid German machine gun fire and our slower 30 caliber machine gun fire. There was a lot of indistinct yelling going on around us while we were burying ourselves. We couldn't see very well as the view in front of us was blocked with heavy brush weighted down with snow. We determined we were in a deep ditch alongside a road parallel to a hedgerow. Nobody else was around, not a soul. It was as scary feeling. We weren't with anyone. We didn't know where we were and we didn't know what happened to the colonel's group. Everybody disappeared!"

"We began hearing cries way off to the left of us calling "Medic". We stood up to try and locate where the cries were coming from but, upon exposing ourselves (and not being camouflaged in white) we drew immediate mortar fire. Mortar fire was systematically aiming and exploding up the hedgerow coming ever closer towards our refuge. One round exploded right in front of us beyond the brush and some of the shrapnel ripped my jacket sleeve. (I was lying on my back at the time.) Now realizing the enemy knew we were there, it was a frightening moment. After that we stayed low and passed the many hours discussing the merits of our hometowns, our favorite foods, schools etc., etc. Towards late afternoon activity had quieted and Tom and I talked about what we should do next. I was in favor of retracing our steps back to town to find Fox Company. Tom was reluctant to leave the relative safety of the ditch. So, I told him I was going back, told him goodbye and jumped up and started running up an incline deep in snow. My progress was slow in the deep snow when all of a sudden I spotted some holes appearing beside me in the snow alongside my shadow. WHAMO!! It dawned on me. I was beingshot at. I was a target! I dropped flat into the snow and began crawling to the crest of the hill. After reaching it, I jumped up and ran back into town where I located some of the guys in our company. I was totally exhausted and mentally wiped out and fell into a deep sleep curled up on some straw in a barn. I never saw Tom after this. I heard he had been diagnosed with trench foot and sent back to medics. He did not return to Fox Company as far as I know."

"My final grim reminder of the Grand Halleux battle was the sight of Graves Registration soldiers loading the frozen Company G casualties into the back end of 6x6 trucks. I had lost many good friends."[26]

The following was S/Sgt Richard R. Debruyn's memory the attack out of Grand Halleaux. "On January 15, Fox moved down hill in the darkness, crossed a makeshift bridge and turned right onto the road into Grand Halleux as a 10 minute barrage rustled over head to crash on the heights to our left. One platoon ahead was hit by enemy shells, wounding several men. 2nd Battalion, 291st Infantry Regiment attacked from Grand Halleux with an exposed left flank. Companies E, G, and H were stopped cold, suffering heavy losses, as did other units. Fox Company was in Battalion reserve. Attacking companies were down to platoon strength by the end of the day. Many spent the day carrying ammunition and wounded. Fox moved up that night to dig in along a fence line. Men crawled about the snow-covered fields searching for survivors. Before day break on the 16th, Companies I and K took over our positions and attacked successfully."[27]

The fact that the Germans stopped the attack of Companies E and G had an effect at the Division level. The book by Trevor Dupuy, *Hitler's last Gamble, the Battle of the Bulge Dec 44 to Jan 45*, describes the relief of the 75th ID Commander. Major General (MG) Ridgway visited the 75th ID CP the day after the attack. Some on MG Ridgway's XVIII Airborne Corps thought the 75th ID commander, MG Prickett, should be relieved of command. Ridgeway wanted to give Prickett another chance. Ridgeway thought the men of the 75th ID had performed well but their leadership was lacking. But when Ridgeway asked Prickett what he needed, Prickett responded "Just pray for me". Ridway took Prickett aside and told him he was relieved because his comment did not inspire confidence.[28] MG Ray Porter was given command of the Division and he stayed in command till the end of the War. Trevor Dupuy's book is one of the few books on the Battle of the Bulge that mentions the actions of the 75th ID.

2nd Battalion was assigned a defensive position at Poteau. Poteau had been taken by 290th Infantry Regiment. 2nd Battalion relieved them that night after a rough march over frozen roads, not knowing exactly where the enemy was. Poteau was on a road that connected to the south east with Saint Vith, a town held by the Germans. The Germans were behind in their schedule for their attack. They had taken Poteau during their attack to the west. Now the Germans were trying to get back to their original lines in the East. 2nd Battalion was trying to keep the Germans bottled up and deny them the use of the East West roadway. The Germans would either break through or have to surrender. The next day at this crossroads, we set up our defenses to coordinate with the rest of the battalion. As usual, LT Cox had the CP in a big barn next to a bigger building, which was used as the Battalion Aid Station. The

Germans wanted this crossroads back as they needed the roads to get some more of their troops out and back to Germany.

Fox received small arms and artillery and mortar fire all day, but our men held off the Germans. We also had some incoming fire from several tanks in the area. Cox went out to check a position held by LT Hanser, Sgt Shelton and several other men. They had a tank positioned in front of an old barn and the men were stationed in and around the barn. The tank would crank up every so often to warm the engine. The tank commander insisted that he had to keep warming the engine in case he had to move the tank. But he probably just wanted to keep warm."

Anyhow, one of the guys spotted a German tank coming around a bend in the road towards us. He pointed it out to the tanker. The gunner held his fire for a few minutes until the German tank got closer and with one round knocked out the tank.

Right afterward the Germans sent an artillery round in on Fox Company. It exploded very close to Cox. He felt the dust biting his legs, but no wounds. LT Hanser got shrapnel in his knee and his shoulder. Irwin Chitwood, the platoon sergeant, used a fireman's carry to take Hanser to the aid station with bullets flying all around. Sgt Shelton and another man got hit with the same shell. A number of men were wounded that day. The Battalion Aid Station was filled with wounded from ours and other units of 2nd Battalion." S/Sgt Bob Berkebile and Pvt Bob Bennish were together in a two man foxhole. An German artillery shell hit near their foxhole. Bennish was killed. Bennish had joined Fox Company from ASTP. S/Sgt Bob Berkebile was badly wounded. Sgt Joe Kirk replaced Bob as the 1st squad leader in 2nd platoon. Nathan Henn was a member of 1st squad and thought Berkebile was also killed. It was not till decades later when both joined the 75th Division Veterans Association, that they learned both had survived the war. Irwin Chitwood recalls that Fox captured 34 Germans during the battle at Poteau.

After night fell, things quieted down. We had held the crossroads. Cox was so tired he couldn't feel it, but sat down in a stall of the barn to have a cup of Nescafe. That's what the K rations called Coffee. Cox reached to pull out his canteen out so he could heat some water over his canned heat. But the canteen wouldn't come out of the cup. After tugging on it awhile, he took off his belt and found a piece of shrapnel had punctured the canteen cup and his canteen, not only locking the canteen in the cup, but spilling out his water. Probably happened when

LT Hanser was hit. A paratrooper, who was relieving Fox, gave Cox some water so he had his Nescafe.

Later the night of January 18th, Fox was relieved by the 517th Parachute Battalion and were we happy to get out of that crossroad town. We moved out in column over a frozen road back toward the vicinity of Grand Halleux. About 2am we pulled into a patch of woods and were told to sack out. Cox was so tired he didn't even dig into the snow. He just threw his sleeping bag on top of it and went to sleep.

About 4am, 1Sgt Sigmund woke Cox up and told him that Capt Drake had selected him to have a 3 day leave to Paris if Cox wanted to go. Cox said ok and promptly went back to sleep since he thought Sigmund was kidding. About 30 minutes later he came back and said Cox had 15 minutes to get to the Battalion CP to catch a truck. Sigmund said leave everything where it was and he'd see that it would be taken care of. Sure enough, when Cox returned about 5 days later someone had taken care of it all. Cox couldn't find a thing that he owned. The worst thing he lost was his carbine, which he had the peep sight filed into a v sight and his trigger squeeze lightened. Never had another one like that afterward. Cox carried a M1 for a long time after that.

The following was written by Capt. Sam Drake describing the feeling after the fight at Poteau. "We had moved up to a crossroad village named Poteau. I don't know how long we were in that position. The road net was an important one for the Germans. The weather was very cold. Most of the men were in exposed positions. There were very few buildings and these had been heavily damaged. Heavy Artillery and mortar fire plus tank harassment caused casualties. The men were bone tired and cold. The relief by the 517th Parachute Infantry was welcomed. I vividly recall that as we were moving back along the snow covered fields and forests how quiet the men were. The silence of the column may have been in part due to extreme fatigue, but also I think, to those thoughts of the recent actions and those that proceeded. Memories of lost buddies, places where those losses occurred, and times when their chances could have gone either way, were on their minds and would remain for a life time"

"I'm sure they were wondering if the green grass and warm sunshine would ever be their good fortune, once more, to share. Somehow I had the feeling as we moved along that night that the men were not despondent. There was a feeling of strength and willingness to go on, knowing that many sacrifices lay ahead."[29]

Ed Letourneau describes the action in which his friend John Klimek was killed at Poteau. The roster of killed and wounded, Appendix A, lists that John was killed on January 18th. But this may be the date the death was recorded on the company morning report. Ed stated in an interview with a local TV station that T/Sgt Chitwood had taken over 3rd Platoon after LT Hanser was wounded. The platoon had to move into part of a town. Chitwood ran across an open area to get to the cover of buildings. Ed was with Chitwood since he was the platoon leader's radio man. Chitwood yelled to his men to run across the open area in a zigzag manner and to not drop to the ground. The Germans had snipers covering the area. Fox men were in olive drab uniforms which stood out against the snow. John Klimek was a big man and was assigned to carry the BAR. John was hit as he crossed the open area. Because of the sniper fire no one could safely go to him till after dark. When John was recovered, he was dead.[30]

S/Sgt Richard R. Debruyn described the fight to control the cross roads at Poteau and later the attack of Aldringen.

"On the night of 16 and 17 January 1945 Fox Company was ordered to supply a combat patrol to the area of Poteau, Belgium. First Platoon (LT Thompson) was selected and the light machine gun section (weapons) was attached. The rest of Fox Company was to follow later with our packs, coats and gear. The patrol was loaded down with extra ammunition, anticipating a skirmish or two."

"The patrol passed through the body-strewn fields of the previous days fiasco and on into the woods where I and K companies had reorganized after their attack. I had to avert my eyes from the bodies of friends I had recognized lying there".

"It became increasingly difficult plodding through the deep drifts. The branches of the trees were covered with about a foot of snow. The avalanche caused by brushing against these sent one staggering to his knees. The extreme cold sapped ones strength. A barking dog had to be dispatched. We wandered those woods for hours growing more exhausted with each dragging step."

"The column finally stopped and I sensed something was wrong. I could hear the LT arguing with someone on the radio. He ordered quiet. We listened and could hear an artillery round burst in the distance. We were lost! I understand the Colonel would not let the patrol return to our lines. They could not correct the course and some time later, came upon a burning village where we were challenged. Fires burned everywhere. It had just been captured by our paratroops (517th). We stood there nervous and jittery as a group advanced to be identified".

"Fox Company and what was left of 2nd Battalion saddled up and moved out over the battlefield down the lumber road toward Petit Their. Two Germans walked out of the woods and surrendered. Our objective was the crossroads of Poteau, Belgium."

"At this time, we did not know how vital this was. The Germans needed to keep it open in order to extricate their remaining troops and rear guard. They fought desperately."

"My recollections of this march are very sparse. On the long move I observed many field pieces in a field to our left. They were of all calibers and poured fire onto the next hill. A makeshift shelter of cartons contained powder bags and I could see men warming themselves about a pot bellied stove inside. Suddenly, a man shot out, his clothing ablaze. One of the nearby loaders tackled and rolled him in the snow, patting out the fire with his hands. I lost sight of them as we turned the bend and went on to Poteau."[31]

The Fox Company followed the patrol in a single file. Capt. Sam Drake was in the lead. LT Cox brought up the rear. Every man was very quiet on this march. At the Poteau crossroads there was a large building, like a warehouse, on one corner. There were several small buildings. On the other side of the road were a barn and a shed about 100 yards from the warehouse. All the buildings, except for the warehouse, were damaged beyond repair. The warehouse was made the company CP. It would later fill up with wounded. Another large building was used as an ammo depot.

S/Sgt Richard R. Debruyn continues his memory of the defense at Poteau. "About daybreak we holed up in a barn near Poteau. A dead German lay in a corner. We learned the 2nd Battalion 290th had just captured the village and we were to relieve them. A short orientation by our Commander let us know there were at least three tanks in the area. We set up a defensive perimeter as dawn broke."

"I helped our other machine gun squad (light 30's) set up a position on the forward slopes that would interlock with fire from my squad. Riflemen and a BAR team formed about this position with protective fire. As I started back, murderous fire drove me to the ground. It took a rather long time to get to my own position, dodging fire all the way. I finally worked my way to the top of the hill and down a ditch to a point just below my gun crew. I spotted a depression and made a mad dash and leap and started digging into the frozen ground. It turned out to be a manure pit. Someone had a bead on me and kept peppering the ground about me. I piled dirt and manure on the downward slope for protection, completed a slit trench, then started digging down for a two man hole. I had about completed this when a body piled in atop of me. I thought "This is it". It turned out to be my section sergeant Cipriani. I was startled to say the least!"

"I was getting fire from my left rear. I had my helmet creased and suspected a sniper in the knocked out tank. By this time we were getting heavy fire from artillery, tanks, machine guns and mortars from the direction of a cluster of houses down the hill to our front. "Cip" took off his shoes and tried to rub life into his badly swollen and discolored feet. He went to Battalion Aid. That was the last I saw of him until our 1971 reunion."

"The incoming fire became intense as they threw everything at us. Any attempt to attack the Germans was stopped cold. Things were getting serious. I spotted two tanks or self propeller antitank guns in a cluster of trees to our left front. They would pop out, fire a few rounds and hide again. I brought fire to bear, but no visible results. We fired on three buildings to our front and later two men were observed carrying wounded along the creek. The incoming fire continued until dark. All we could do was sit it out."

"LTC Drain was going by the building used as an ammo depot in his jeep. He saw a half track parked by the depot loaded with ammo and it was on fire. He quickly decided the halftrack had to be moved. If it exploded with all the ammo in its hull, the ammo depot would go up in a massive explosion. LTC Drain jumped in the half track and drove it far enough away to where he thought the ammo depot would be safe. He jumped off the half track and it ran about 50 yards before exploding. For his quick thinking and actions with disregard for his own safety, LTC Drain was awarded the Silver Star. If he hadn't driven the vehicle away from the ammo depot, it would have blown up and there would have been loss of lives."

"The 2nd Battalion, 517th Paratroops relieved Fox about 2am. They removed our wounded as we moved down the road to Grand Halleux, to where our cooks had set up a chow line. LT Hanser was being evacuated by jeep. He had a knee and shoulder wound."

"We were all subdued by the day's pounding and the loss of close comrades. The column was very quiet, each man lost in his own thoughts as we trudged back to an area near Grand Halleux. We had survived another day!"[32]

Gathering of Fox men at Grand Halleux. Pvt William Crawford standing at the left, Cpl Ray Stoddard sitting third from the left, Sgt Fulsom standing by himself on the right fore ground.[33]

S/Sgt Richard R. Debruyn continued. "Suddenly, Grand Halleux had become a bustling village. Heavy artillery and other support units had moved in. The 106th Infantry Division had been pinched off and was preparing to move out of the sector."

"Fox Company received last minute orders, after a brief rest, to move to the Division's extreme right sector to be attached to with 3rd battalion 291st Infantry. Fox Company was apart of the XVIII Corps attack south to cut off the routes of retreat for the Germans from the Bulge. We moved by truck and relieved units of the 289th Infantry. A hot chow line had been set up and after eating, the Company moved into positions in the woods and prepared to attack the following morning. We were to clear out pockets of resistance and capture the village of Aldringen, southeast of Saint Vith."[34] ."

According to the actions against the enemy report for January, Fox was attached to 3rd Battalion while the rest of 2nd Battalion was in reserve and reorganizing after the losses on January 15th. Fox led the attack by 3rd Battalion. Resistance was slight and the Regiment gained 3500 yards during the day of January 22nd.

Debruyn continued, "The morning of January 21st the Company dropped packs and bedrolls and moved out through dense thickets. Progress was slow at first."

"Breaking, at last, into the clear, several deer were flushed ahead of us. We caught fire from the knoll beyond, which was quickly beaten down by our leading platoon. Moving forward cautiously, we encountered more rear guard troops. Eventually, we came to a road through the forest clearing, where we received heavy fire from an under strength company. Fox Company held up close to the road and an artillery concentration was called in. One short round hit the top of a tall tree and showered our men with heavy branches. Fortunately, no one was hurt. Our riflemen flushed out about ten survivors. I can still hear the pitiful calls of "Sani" in the deep silence following that concentration. (sani means medic in German) I remember the platoon sergeant telling the Germans being bandaged by our Medics "Damit it! You should have stopped when I yelled Halt! It's your own damned fault!""

"The Company was near the edge of the woods when we were strafed by our own planes. Three tanks were observed jockeying about the crest of a vast crescent shaped barren ridge to our front. An air strike was called and rockets soon had the three ablaze. Men dashed to this area and set up a perimeter near the hulks as the rest of the Battalion moved up".

"Darkness fell as we continued along this ridge and soon encountered more Germans in a farm building. Two heavy machine guns went into action, spraying the area. Some of our tanks moved up alongside us while other troops attacked across our front. Return fire appeared as twinkling fireflies in the darkness. We set off again with no further opposition".

"Dawn found Fox Company skidding on ice ponds in a watershed area near a destroyed rail station. We were fatigued. I can still see Captain Drake leaning against a tree cussing his heart out! Tracer fire licked all about us. The Company moved across the railroad tracks and into a wooded area. We found freshly evacuated dugouts which were warm and comfortable and gave protection from the artillery concentrations. The Company spent the night and next day here."

"The night of the 23rd, one of our patrols was ambushed near Aldringen. Sgt Glasscock and Winebrenner (a close friend) were killed. I can still hear Sgt Moss near our hole calling for volunteers to help evacuate the boys. We formed a hasty patrol and took our squad's machine gun to set up a base of fire while they were checked out. The fire was too heavy and the bodies were left were they fell. Years later a sergeant from I Company told me that Germans in tanks kept riding over them while taunting his company to come out and fight. I have reservations about this story".

"The morning of the 24th, our Company moved along the perimeter of this woods and encountered trip wires. I believe they were frozen tight as they failed to explode. The column moved to the right through Beho to catch Aldringen on the flank. I can still see the machine gun bullets kicking up snow about the attacking platoons as they charged across the open fields. Heavy mortar, tank, and machine gun fire soon pinned down the Company at the edge of the village. One tank came down the road, close to where we cowered in the ditch, and sprayed the area with machine gun fire".

"A company of Germans with tank support was observed forming for an attack at the rear of the village. No one was moving, so I dashed across the road and moved down the slope, in defilade, to get to the farm house, without incident, via the barn. I took one prisoner, who was shot dead before he took 5 steps".

"Peering through an ustairs window, I immediately drew fire from positions along a fence line about one hundred yards or so away. Signaling my machine gun squad to come to me, I had my crew pour fire into this area. We were also getting fire from some of the buildings beyond. I still had not cleared the house or barn, nor the German machine gun nest across the street". I went back to call for more ammunition and found part of Headquarters and 1st platoon in the barn drinking milk and eating bread and preserves the farmer had. About fifteen women and children were crouched in the stables near the kitchen door".

"About this time, I heard Captain Drake had been shot. He was shot in the hip. The round ruptured and coursed up along his spine. I went back with two rifle non-coms and cajoled and threatened some attached tanks to help us evacuate him. They poured fire into several buildings, then moved up. I helped lift his litter onto one of the tanks. He was so still and white-faced! I vowed aloud to get the German who shot him. One of the rifle squads evened the score before I got back to the farm house. Things quieted down after a bit".

"After dark, Fox Company moved in with fighting at close quarters and some hand-to-hand. The Germans filtered in behind us and bodies piled in the streets. I remember one of our lads was so concerned with his groin that he forgot to mention the several bullet holes in his stomach. Before the medic found these, he had bled to death. We lost a lot of good boys here. Eventually the village was cleared and 3rd Battalion moved in to take up positions".

"Shortly after dawn, I stood on a knoll when three sharp blasts blew me into a ditch. I had a brief glimpse of a tank or SP before I passed out. Hours later our medic carried me piggy-back to the Battalion Aid Station in a corner of a house. They pumped morphine into me and I was evacuated by ambulance. This ended my career as a combat man. Eleven months later, I was discharged 50% combat disabled from Camp Butner General Hospital".[35]

Capt Drake was wounded while moving towards the German tanks. Drake had called for the bazooka man to come forward. The man was so afraid, Drake took the bazooka. As he set out to get the tank, he was shot.

T/Sgt Pappy French was the platoon sergeant of 2nd platoon. He had served in combat in Alaska fighting the Japanese in the Aleutian Islands. T/Sgt French was not afraid of anything. He stood in the middle of the street in Aldringen firing his M1 at Germans up on the ridge.

According to the actions against the enemy report for January, the attack on Aldringen started in the early afternoon against heavy resistance. The town was completely in hand by 8:35 pm, "after characteristic village fighting". To veterans of World War II characteristic village fighting speaks volumes.

On January 25, 1945 the 75th ID made the headlines of the *Stars and Stripes*. The article states the 75th ID had taken Audrange, which is an alternative spelling of the town of Aldringen, Belgium. Towns in Belgium had French and Flemish names. The article stated the Germans had 5 tanks and 100 infantrymen and they gave heavy resistance. The article stated the 75th ID attack at Audrange along with the 1st ID and 7th Armored Division attacks vicinity Saint Vith severed the north south spokes of the Saint Vith road hub.[36]

Used with permission from Stars and Stripes © 1945, 2012 Stars and Stripes.

On the back page of this issue of the *Stars and Stripes*, it was reported that French troops were attacking north of Colmar to gain the initiative against the German thrust toward Strasbourg. Also the *Stars and Stripes* reported the 6th Army was advancing against the Japanese on the Island of Luzon in the Philippines and Saipan based Super fortress B-29 bombers attacked main land Japan.[37]

From January 19th to January 25th, seven men from Fox Company were killed. Pvt Benish was killed by an artillery round. PFC Hugh McDermott was hit by rifle or machine gun fire while firing his Browning Automatic Rifle (BAR) at the Germans. S/Sgt Donnie Glasscock and PFC James Winebrenner were killed by small arms fire. PFC Klimek and PFC Bert Nelson were killed at Aldringen. PFC Ridley Meeks died of wounds suffered at Poteau.

During this time twenty one men were wounded. Long stays in hospital awaited these men. As an example, S/Sgt Robert Berkebile needed bone grafts and he spent over two years in Army hospitals.[38]

It is a common occurrence that infantry men discarded equipment that they did not think they needed to lighten the load they had to carry. In Belgium, Hank Arend tossed aside his mess kit. "I thought just get rid of it. It's too much to haul around. The fighting was so intense that we rarely got a warm meal, so what use of that mess kit? We ate K rations instead". In 2004 Hank's grandson, Jesse Babbitz, was looking on the computer for his grandfather's email. The name Hank Arend came up on a site of a World War II equipment collector in Belgium who was selling a mess kit with Hank Arend scratched on the bottom. Jesse contacted the seller and bought the mess kit. The seller bought the mess kit from another collector so he did not know how the mess kit was found. It was clearly Hank's mess kit since it had his service number as well as his name scratched on the bottom. Jokingly Hank told Jesse, "I threw it away 60 years ago. Now what would I want with it now?" The mess kit allowed Jesse to connect with his grandfather and his past.[39]

Hand Arend with his mess kit.
IJ photo/Frankie Frost

LT Cox was able to spend three days in Paris, with other officers and men from 291st Regiment. He mostly stayed in bed and slept. He arrived at the 2nd Battalion CP to learn that Capt Drake had been wounded. LT Harvey Cannon, 2nd Platoon leader, had taken command during the final stage of the battle of Aldringen. After the battle of Aldringen, Fox Company had three officers and 65 men. Fox Company had arrived in Europe with 6 officers and 190 men. Many men were injured by the cold weather, suffering frost bit, snow blindness and trench foot. On arrival in Europe the 75th Division was called by some the diaper division, because its average age was so young. While Fox Company had lost many men, the ones that were left were seasoned combat men.

All soldiers liked to get mail. Family and friends would send letters keeping the soldier abreast of news back home. Often they would send packages of cookies, peanuts or other types of snack food. Soldiers in combat could use V mail. The soldier would get one sheet of paper. All letters were read by a censor so you could not write about the situation in Europe. The letters in the combat zone had to be written plainly and clearly. The letters would be photo copied and reduced to 4 inches by 5 inches. This was done to reduce the bulk size of mail. Initially soldier's mail was sent to England to be processed and reduced. In February 1945, mail was processed in Paris. The letters were placed on a reel of film and sent to New York, Chicago or San Francisco to be printed out. Not all mail was reduced. Some letters from soldiers went in a standard sized envelope and paper and posted with a 6 cent airmail stamp.

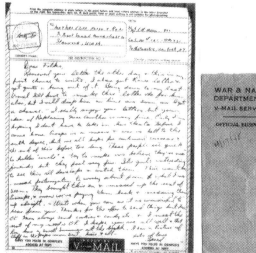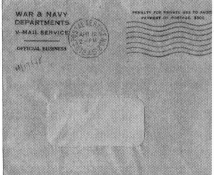

Example of V-Mail, Earl Adams to Aunt and Uncle[40]

As stated earlier, Cpl Ray Stoddard was armed with Springfield 1903 A3 rifle with a scope. The hardest part of the war for him "was trying to load the darn thing with cold and numb hands. The worst thing can happen is to be caught with an empty weapon." But he did not start out as a sniper or a member of the Company headquarters. This is his story of how he ended up with the sniper rifle during the war.

"My having the sniper rifle has a story. It starts with Wales. I was an assistant squad leader in Sgt. Russ Kime's squad. I got a pass to go to London in November. After arriving there I felt like I had the flu so went to a city aid station to get some pills or something that would help during my time there. There was lone doctor there, a Major, who told me that I was going to the hospital and I immediately told him I was on leave and didn't intend to go. His retort was "you are going and that is an order" so I was put in an ambulance and shipped off to a hospital somewhere in London. My first night there I was beginning to wonder why I was there. This my first experience in hearing the loud booms of the V-2 rockets coming in and it was scary thing. The doctors in the hospital kept me there for at least three weeks and they didn't know what was wrong or wouldn't tell me. I was the only guy in the ward not wounded. All the others were badly damaged soldiers coming from the hedgerows and I felt so bad for them as many weren't going to make it. Anyway, I somehow learned that the 75th ID was on the move to Southampton. I wrangled a release and was sent to the 10th replacement depot in mid England which was a hell hole (former British troop barracks, very cold damp and miserable.) The place was run by Colonel Killian, whom I read later, was court marshaled for being cruel to soldiers."

"Upon arrival, I was on the docket to be shipped to the mainland of Europe as a replacement. Distraught and in tears, I met with the camp chaplain and pleaded to return to the 75th ID. He took pity on me and saw to it that I had the necessary traveling papers to return to my unit at the Southampton docks. After a long train ride, I checked in with Capt. Drake and found that they had stored all my stuff somewhere else as they hadn't expected me back. So there I was in my dress woolens and no other gear and boarded the vessel that way. I was replaced and no longer in my squad. Upon arrival at LeHarve we climbed down the nets to a LSD and boated to the dock. I scrounged for equipment and ended up with the 1903-A3 w/scope. And that's how I became a sniper. I was a pretty good marksman having acquired expert medals when stationed at Fort Bliss. I had shot at pop up targets while walking, crawling and running on a mountain trails in the foothills of an El Paso mountain. So that's the story. I wasn't called upon to be a sniper officially. It just happened and I was carried on the company roster as kind of a odd man out. Kime's squad disintegrated after being in Belgium and that's when we were broken up into combat teams assigned to the 2nd tank guys. I wasn't actually a part of headquarters; Captain Drake kept me close by. I carried the 300 radio occasionally and did other duties. I just tried to fill in where needed. I didn't like patrols and tried to be invisible when plans were laid to send guys out. But it didn't always work. I ended up with my fair share of patrol duty."[41]

In most history books concerning the Battle of the Bulge, mention of the 75th ID either states the Division was green, lacking combat experience, or the books state the attack by the 75th was slow. These historians overlook the contributions of the 75th ID's Infantry Regiments supporting the 2nd and 3rd Armored Divisions stopping the western attack of the Germans. The historians rightly state the 75th ID was green but they overlook that their German opponents were combat veterans, many from the eastern front fighting for 2 years against the Russians. The 75th ID and Fox Company should be proud of their accomplishments in their first battles.

COLMAR POCKET

★ ★ ★

Bullets were so close they were clipping small limbs of bushes over Chitwood's head. Cox told Chitwood not to rise up or he would be dead.

WITH THE BATTLE OF Aldringen completed, Fox Company's combat in the Battle of the Bulge was over. There was a plan to send the 75th ID to Liege, Belgium for a rest, reorganization and for replacements. Instead on January 25th the Division was sent hundreds of miles by train to the vicinity of Colmar, France. The Germans had attacked there and created another bulge, this time in France. Review of Military History books gives some insight why the 75th ID was sent to Colmar. After the German's had lost the Battle of the Bulge, General Eisenhower wanted General Bradley to send a Corps with four Divisions to attack the Germans in the Colmar Pocket. The majority of the Allied Army forces around Colmar were French and US Divisions (the 3rd Infantry Division and the 36th Infantry Division) that had made the attack into Southern France from the Riviera on August 15, 1944 in Operation Dragoon. General Omar Bradley wrote in his book, *A General's Life*, that he strongly objected to striping his Army Group of a Corps, because it would hold up Bradley's plan to attack into Germany. In the end Bradley won. Troops, that were the reserves for the Supreme Headquarters Allied Expeditionary Forces (SHAEF), were sent to Colmar[42] The 28th ID and the 75th ID had just been pulled off the line after the Battle of the Bulge to rest and receive badly needed replacements. The 28th ID and the 75th ID became part of SHAEF"s reserves. Thus the 28th and the 75th were available to be sent to Southern France to attack the Colmar Pocket.

At the beginning of December 1945 the 291st Infantry Regiment landed in Europe, it had 153 officers, 5 warrant officers and 3031enlisted men.[43] At the beginning of February, the 291st Infantry Regiment had 121 officers, 5 warrant officers and 2189 enlisted men.[44] After the Battle of the Bulge Fox Company had 3 officers, Cox, Cannon and Thompson, and 90 men. But these men were battle harden tough bunch, who knew how to fight the Germans. Nathan Henn recalled that Fox had learned during the Battle of the Bulge that they could take casualties and not fall apart. Through out the Battle of the Bulge, Fox did not receive replacements. Henn stated in an interview with his Grandson Richard Krosin, that you found more strength within you and you did your job. Even though we had half our strength, we were pushing the Germans back and that helped our morale.[45].

The trains the troops traveled in to Colmar, France had been used to haul German prisoners. There was hay on the floor and it was dark. The POW's had used the corners of the box cars as their bathroom and this mess had not been cleaned out.

The 291st Infantry Regiment detrained and assembled in the woods near Weidwihr, France on January 30th.[46] The 291st moved to the little town of Fortschwihr and bivouacked in civilian houses. This area of France seemed to like the Germans better than the Americans. The 75th ID was assigned to a French Army at this time. Ed Letourneau had learned French in Elementary school and High School and was used as a Company interpreter with the French and also earlier in Belgium. In the Company Ed was called "Frenchie".[47]

Fox Company CP was in the basement of a large house which was attached to a dairy barn with cows and manure. There was a very large wine barrel full of red wine and lots of white wine in bottles. The barrel must have been built in the basement because it was too big to move. At first we would not drink any of the wine because we wanted to have clear heads when we got orders to move. We stayed there a couple of days just staring at that wine and wishing. On January 31st, 10 soldiers from Fox Company were wounded and one killed , mostly from German artillery.

On January 31st at 2 am, company commanders were called to the battalion CP for further orders. The 75th ID was to go on the attack on February 1st 1945 along with the 3rd Infantry Division.

2nd Battalion was to lead the regimental attack, followed by 1st Battalion. LTC Drain gave us our orders to attack the next morning.

Fox Company objective was the railroad station. We had to attack across the road through the woods to get to the railroad station. This would be Ted Cox's first attack in command of the company. The men wondered how he would perform.

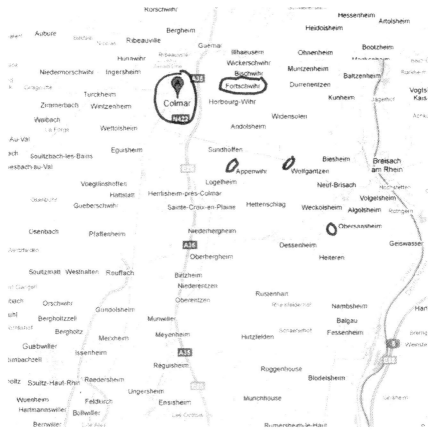

Google Map of Colmar, France[48]
Fox's first CP was in Fortswihr just to the east of Colmar. The 75th and Fox Company attacked to the southeast towards the towns of Appenwihr, Wolfgantzen and Obersaaheim, all marked with a black circle.

The Company was divided in to three rifle platoons of 21 men each. LT Thompson would lead 1st platoon. LT Cannon would lead 2nd platoon. T/Sgt Chitwood would lead 3rd Platoon. S/Sgt Porter would lead weapons platoon with 10 men light machine gun section and one 60 mm mortar.

After all this was done Cox called Thompson, Cannon, Chitwood, and Porter into the CP and gave them his orders for the attack the next morning. There would be a 6 minute artillery barrage at 6 minutes before 7 am. At precisely 7 am, we would cross the road in a skirmish line and continue through the woods, clearing whatever Germans would get in our way until we reached the railroad station. Porter would follow closely if we should need the extra firepower. It was thought the Germans would put up a stronger fight to hold the railroad station than in the woods. That turned out to be right on both counts.

The leaders synchronized their watches at about 9 pm. Then they tried the wine, just a few glasses. The red wine was sweet and delicious. The white wine was dry.

The next morning February 1st at 7 am the attack went off just as planned. A small group of Germans were holding the road when the artillery barrage began. Glimpses of a few wearing white uniforms were seen running away. Three of the ones that survived the artillery threw down their rifles and were running around like crazy, stunned by the artillery blasts. Cox told the men to fix bayonets and stick them if they did not stop. They did not understand English but they understood what the bayonets meant and they stopped running. Cox sent the three prisoners back to battalion with one man to escort them. After he delivered them he was to come back and catch up with the company. We resumed our advance through the woods. In a few moments we heard three shots. A few minutes later the guard came back. He said the three Germans tried to escape and he had to kill them. The guard probably remembered back in the Ardennes we were told to take no prisoners because the Germans had taken about 120 Americans prisoner at Malmedy, Belgium, lined them up and deliberately machine gunned them to death. The Germans did not know some of the men survived and got back to our lines and told what had happened. The account of what happened spread through the whole US Armies. There is no way to know how many German troops would have survived the war if they had not killed the American prisoners at Malmedy.

Not taking prisoners may have been a problem through out the Army. The *Stars and Stripes* had a full page story in the January 28, 1945 issue on the importance of taking prisoners and the intelligence that trained interrogators could get out of the German prisoners.[49]

Cox decided the men needed something besides water. So PFC Hank Arend was sent back to the old CP to bring two Jerry cans of wine. Arend got back with the wine and all the men and officers had wine with their hot meal.

That worked out so well, Cox sent Arend back the next day for more wine to go with the hot meal. Hank drove back and got more wine. On the way back to the diner site, the jeep came under artillery fire. Arend drove on through the fire and got through safely. But the wine did not fair so well. The Jerry cans strapped to the sides of the jeep were punctured and all the wine had leaked out.

After the attack had progressed, 1st Battalion which had been following 2nd Battalion, side slipped to the left and attacked in the left sector of the Regiment.

At Approximately 2 pm, troops of the German 19th Assault Battalion counterattack against 2nd Battalion. The enemy initially gained 500 yards. During the counterattack, Cox, T/Sgt Chitwood and T/Sgt French were in a gully with machine gun bullets popping overhead. In fact the bullets were so close they were clipping small limbs off the bushes over Chitwood's head. Cox told Chitwood not to rise up or he would be dead.

Fox had one bazooka, which the company commander kept under his control. The commander would take it to the platoon that needed it. During the counterattack, Cox heard a tank coming. Because of the wooded area, they could not tell if it was a German tank. Cox called for the bazooka. T/Sgt French took the weapon, since was one of the best in the company with the bazooka. Cox acted as the loader. French aimed and Cox put in the rocket projectile. They were ready to fire. The tank was getting closer and they still could not see it. Suddenly the tank appeared and the first thing they saw was the big white star on the front. Cox and French breathed a sigh of relief. By 5:30 pm the Germans were completely repulsed and 2nd Battalion continued the attack.

On February 1st as 2nd Battalion prepared defensive positions. The 291st Regimental overlay showed 1st and 2nd Battalions defending side by side with 2nd Battalion on the right. In the 2nd Battalion sector, Companies F and G were side by side with Company E in reserve.

Fox continued the attack through the woods, meeting only light resistance. 2nd Battalion was positioned along the Neuf Brisach-Andolsheim Road. Night came and we had to stop our advance. We were in the middle of the French fortification called the Maginot Line. After World War I, the French thought they would build a line of fortifications along the German French boarders. They thought they could defend themselves much better if the Germans ever attacked them again. When World War II began, it was a whole new ball game. The Germans were armed with tanks so they rolled over and around the French fortifications and in six weeks the French surrendered.

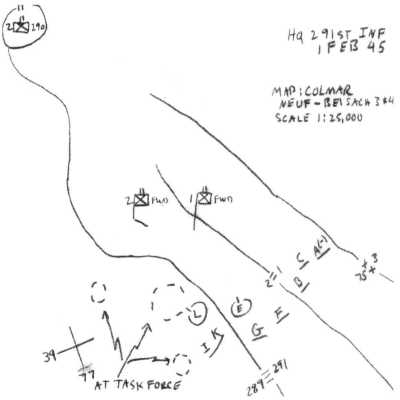

291st Infantry Regiment Overlay dated 1 February 1945[50]

Since we were in the middle of these fortifications, we decided to make use of them. To house the French troops they built a series of bunkers, thick concrete covered with earth. There were five bunkers built together with a concrete trench in front so the occupants could exit the bunkers and still have the cover of being under ground level.

Each bunker was equipped with three double bunk beds, with plenty of room for more troops to sleep in their sleeping bags on the floor. The front door was built of thick wood and heavy. We occupied five bunkers, all the men in four bunkers, except in LT Cox's bunker, LT Thompson, T/Sgt Chitwood, and five others. We left one man outside to warn us of any approaches.

The Germans had a rocket firing device called nebelwerfers. They would fire one every few minutes not aimed at any target, just hoping to hit something. The rocket would leave the launcher, making a swooshing noise. The rockets were loaded with a lot of high explosives and would do lots of damage when they hit.

The Germans must have thought someone would be occupying the bunkers because the rockets were landing real close. Pvt James Reid was on guard when a rocket landed in the trench a few feet from Cox's bunker. It knocked a large chunk of concrete into Reid killing him instantly. The blast from the explosion blew the wooden door of our bunker off and a large wood splinter hit LT Thompson's right arm causing a wound that sent him to the hospital. He recuperated from that wound and rejoined the company about April 7th, the day after the Rutgers Castle battle.

The Regiment had gained 3000 yards on February 1st. But a gap was evident between the right flank of the 291st Regiment and the 289th Regiment. Plans were made for the Regimental Anti Tank Company to occupy blocking positions.

On February 2nd the Regiment defended the ground gained. During the day the 289th Regiment was counter attacked and force to leave Appenwihr. 2nd Battalion was alerted for movement to right flank of the Regiment should any enemy thrust come from Appenwihr. Meanwhile 2d Battalion extensively patrolled the right flank to maintain contact with the 289th Regiment.

Early the next morning we resumed our attack toward the railroad station. When we got within sight of the station, we observed German troops in strength guarding the station.

LT Cannon wanted the job of taking the station so he got the mission to assault. Cannon with his men sneaked up on the Germans, surprising them and after a short firefight, what was left of the German troops surrendered.

On February 3rd, Fox Company continued the attack vicinity Fortschwihr with a battalion objective of Wolfgantzen. We took the woods to move to open ground overlooking Wolfgantzen. We held up there for further orders. The past three days we were constantly bombarded with rockets and artillery fire. Enemy shelling was intense. Sgt William Welch and PFC William Evans were killed by artillery fire.

When we moved up to the edge of the woods overlooking Wolfgantzen, there was an old bunker with a badly wounded German soldier. His arm was swelled up and he must have been several days without medical attention. The company aid man did not want to treat him because it would be a waste of medical supplies since the German was going to die anyway. Cox ordered him to treat the German's wounds and he did. The German was so grateful. Cox took the German's wrist watch and gold chain from around his neck.

Early the next morning, we found the German dead on the road. He had had a gold ring on his finger. He was missing his ring finger and the gold ring. Someone had cut off his finger to get the ring. Whoever reads this don't get excited over what had happened. It happened on both sides. We learned this from the Germans.

Fox got orders to pull back 300 yards into the woods. We did not know why. That was par for the course. We never knew where we were until we read about it in the *Stars and Stripes*.

Fox stayed in the woods for three days under constant artillery and rocket fire. LTC Drain ordered Fox to a crossroad, three quarters of a mile east of us, and support a tank that was there. Fox went through the woods and found the tank. We set up defensive positions. The only thing we encountered that night was artillery fire and there were no casualties.

The 291st Infantry Regiment overlay for February 5th Showed Companies L, G and F defending side by side with Company F on the left facing southeast. Company E was to the rear facing west to cover an attack route the Germans might take. 1st Battalion occupies a battalion position in the Regimental sector.

LTC Drain gave Fox orders to attack the town of Wolfgantzen. It was suppose to be a night attack. At 4 pm the Air Corps was suppose to hit Wolfgantzen with bombs and at 6 pm artillery was suppose to start. Then Fox was to go in and take the town. We had not been trained for night fighting. But a soldier takes orders and carries them out to the best of their abilities. During the afternoon Fox trained themselves on how to identify each other at night. We were all relieved when they called off the attack.

German planes were flying overhead and dropping bombs on 2nd Battalion. American planes were bombing the bridge over the Rhine River. The flak was so heavy that they did not get close to the bridge.

On February 4th, 3rd Battalion with 2nd Battalion following continued to attack to seize Wolgantzen. The 3rd and 2nd Battalion ended the day occupying defensive positions west of Wolfgantzen. 1st Battalion moved north of the town. The Germans were expecting an attack from the west and were taken by surprise when 1st Battalion attacked from the north. 1st Battalion stayed in Wolfgantzen as the Division reserve. 2nd Battalion was attached to the 290th Infantry Regiment and moved to Obersaasheim. 2nd Battalion established road blocks and sent patrols towards the Rhine River.

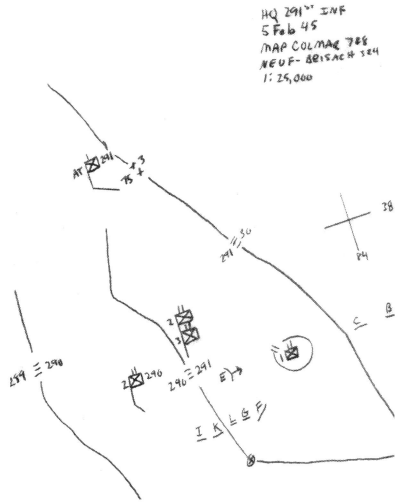

291st Infantry Regiment Overlay dated 5 February 1945[51]

By February 6th, 2nd Battalion was at Obersaaheim within sight of the Rhine River. 2nd Battalion mounted an attack against the German strong point. Easy Company had lost their company commander a few days before and a captain from battalion headquarters wanted a taste of combat so LTC Drain let him lead Easy Company. Fox was in reserve. Easy went about a quarter of a mile when they came under small arms and mortar fire. The battle lasted several hours and from all the noise of the battle the battle was moving toward Fox,

LT Cox had carried an M1 Garand rifle since he lost his carbine. Cox took some grenades and went German hunting. He sneaked around through the woods toward all the firing, thinking he might find one of the German machine gun crews. If Cox got lucky he would toss a grenade on them and open up with the M1 and wipe them out. Cox was dreaming of course, it never happened. While sneaking around in the woods, he saw LTC Drain sneaking around with his 45 automatic drawn. They met and Cox asked Drain "What are you doing out here?" Drain said, "Probably the same thing you are doing out here." Then they went their separate ways German hunting.

The Germans must have known there were American soldiers in those woods because not too long after running into Drain, Cox heard an artillery shell coming in. It does not take long under shell fire until you can tell by the sound whether the shell is going to be short or long or whether its coming to your side. The shell landed about 200 yards short. The second landed about 200 yards long. Cox knew he was bracketed and the next round would be on top of him. Sure enough he heard it coming and he hugged the ground, knowing by the sound it was right on him. The shell plowed into the ground about 15 or 20 feet away and it threw dirt all over him. But it did not explode. Cox thanked God for letting the Germans put a slave laborer where he or she could sabotage that shell. Stephen Ambrose in "Citizen Soldiers" wrote that after forty years of interviewing World War II veterans he found Americans often talked about German artillery rounds failing to explode. But the German veterans never talked about American artillery duds. Ambrose stated this was the difference between free American laborers versus German slave laborers, some who found a way to sabotage the artillery rounds.

Easy Company had won their battle and was coming back along the road with a good number of prisoners. Cox will never forget the sight of the captain with a million dollar wound, being brought out on a stretcher. He was cussing the prisoners as they walked along beside him. He was lying on the stretcher with his 45 caliber pistol in his hand when suddenly he raised his pistol and fired a shot right up beside a German's ear. He was so mad he would not have cared if he had shot the guy's head off.

Finally the bulge was flattened. The Germans had retreated across the Rhine. After fighting in the Battle of the Bulge and the Colmar Pocket, the 75th Infantry Division was called the Bulge Busters.

After a day of rest and cleaning equipment, we were told we were going to get a shower. We went to the shower tents and had to take off our clothes and leave them. Everyman got 5 minutes to soap up and finish his shower. We left on the other side of the tent where we were given new clothes. Needless to say we all felt a lot better after the shower and clean clothes. The Rhineland campaign was behind us. At the end of the Colmar pocket Fox had just 2 officers and 65 men.

Dick Forni wrote the following in a letter to Capt Sam Drake in 1987. Dick had been a military policeman for 18 months. His MP company at Fort Lewis disbanded and the soldiers were sent to the 75th ID to be infantrymen. Dick wrote that after the battle at Aldringen, there were only three men left in his squad in 1st platoon. Dick was made a S/Sgt and squad leader. Bob Wallace was made Sgt and assistant squad leader. The third man was Pvt Brenner.

Dick wrote the following about the fight in the Colmar Pocket. "On one patrol (day light) S/Sgt Reagan, who was leading the patrol, was badly wounded in the foot. S/Sgt Reagan was platoon guide for 1st platoon. There were four of us on the patrol. S/Sgt Reagan, myself and PFC's Brenner and Tito. We were going along a trail behind a fairly high embankment and thought we were safe from enemy observation. But one enemy observer evidently could see us very plainly. Four artillery pieces opened up on us. They had to aim high to clear the embankment. But even so, shrapnel was flying all around us. I thought for sure that we would all be killed or wounded. Reagan called out suddenly and said he had been hit. I managed to get over to him, called Brenner to help me and sent Tito to get a medic. The German guns stopped firing. Why that happened I don't know but I was very glad that it did, because I was able to help Reagan in the way I explained. Tito came back with a medic, who gave Reagan a shot in the foot and then we took Reagan back to the Company area, put him on a jeep and sent him back to the hospital".

"Another time, when the company was advancing through a thinly wooded forest, enemy artillery opened up on us. PFC Goldman, who was in another squad, started calling for help. He was about 50 yards from me, but I was able to work my way over to him. Again there was that slit in the shoe, just like Reagan's, from shrapnel. This time, I called for a company medic, who worked his way over to us and took care of Goldman, while I went back to my original position"[52]

Colmar it was cold but there was less snow. Cold weather injuries still occurred. S/Sgt Earl Adams got frost bite on his toes. His toes turned black and he was hospitalized. The doctors wanted to amputate the toes. Earl told them to go cut off their own toes. Luckily his toes returned to normal. Earl was to go to a replacement center but he went AWOL from the hospital and hitch hiked to Holland to link up went Fox Company.

Corporal Ray Stoddard had the following memory of the fighting in the Colmar Pocket.

"Soon after, we were collected in a rail yard and entrained again on those infamous French boxcars, 40 & 8's (forty men or 8 horses) for a cold, miserably foul smelling and uncomfortable two-day ride to central France somewhere near the Vosges Mountains. Previous fighting through those mountains had compressed and contained the German troops into what was nicknamed "The Colmar Pocket". The Germans were surrounded by Allied troops whose mission was to prevent them from crossing the nearby Rhine River."

"From the train we were loaded into 6 by 6 trucks and driven to a wooded area where we spent a few days thawing out and drawing replacement equipment. There was a damp spring-like warmth in the air and our spirits were lifted by this change after so many weeks of bone-chilling cold. While we were living in this woods some of the guys did a little deer hunting. One man displayed his marksmanship by bagging a deer. Sgt. Shelton dressed it out and shared portions of this delicacy with many of us. I barely finished cooking my portion when we received orders to move out. Believe me, a hastily fried hunk of venison still tasted like the finest steak after so many months of GI rations."

"After Captain Drake was wounded, the company executive officer, LT Cox, became our new company commander. My first contact with his leadership was one very dark night as the men were being placed along a defensive line in these thick woods. He was leading us through these woods by following a compass; the night was so dark one could barely see two feet in front. We were lined up single file and followed each other as best we could, often stumbling in the dark. We would pause about every twenty feet, drop off a rifleman and then go on to the next drop off point. After I was positioned, I began to dig a foxhole and immediately ran into thick tangled roots close to the surface which prevented me from digging very deep. Sitting in my shallow hole and surrounded by the inky darkness was an eerie experience. It was impossible to see anything looking straight forward but by peering to the side one could just make out different shapes. I am fairly certain that an enemy patrol penetrated our lines that night but no one challenged them and we all held our fire. I had a perception of human forms silently walking around ahead of me but in the deep darkness I couldn't be certain. Possibly it was my imagination."

"My next memory was in the same woods but in daylight. We had reformed and were pushing through this forest entanglement of thick understory. Again it was very difficult to see very far ahead. I did attempt to count the number of men positioned in our line and came up with a number of 23...not many to be effective against the enemy. We had one lone machine gunner, a weapons platoon sergeant carrying a water-cooled thirty caliber machine gun with his shoulders wrapped with his links of ammunition. He had no ammo bearer. Although a heavy load for him, he was cheerful as he walked along and his upbeat attitude encouraged us all. During this foray we encountered a tank ahead of us. I couldn't see it but could hear the rumble just ahead. We stopped to figure our next move. We weren't equipped with a bazooka, only rifle grenades. We knew those wouldn't do the job if that tank were to turn towards us. As we stood there listening, the engine exhaust noise faded away. We had averted that crisis. Since it was turning dark, we held up there."

"We were seldom briefed on the battle plans, but somehow we knew that our goal was liberating a walled city, Neuf Brisach. Later, looking at this town after the fighting was over, I could see what a challenge it would had been for our understaffed company. It was a thickly bricked fortress encircled by a moat and portals armed with heavy artillery. As it turned out, we didn't have to capture that fortress as elements of the 3rd ID took it."

"Imprinted indelibly on my mind is a memory of the night we spent in these woods around Neuf Brisach. Scattered in the forest were remnants of pillboxes of a former enemy defensive line. We came under heavy artillery fire that night and we all sought out any kind of protection we could find. Some of us ducked into a concrete entrance to one of these pillboxes. Settled into this cement entrance with tree branches crashing and shrapnel sizzling, I faced a "big" decision. Through all the fighting I had been carefully protecting and preserving a Mason jar filled with breast of pheasant that my dad had shot while on a hunting trip in South Dakota and my mom and grandma had lovingly canned and shipped to me. I had received it at the last mail call. Figuring that this just might be a "last meal," I unscrewed the top and shared the delicacy with the guys around me. Luck was with us that night when we chose the shelter we did. Some of the others weren't as lucky and their pillbox took a direct hit."

"The next day we were still in the forest and advancing under heavy overhead artillery fire. I was walking with my buddy, Jerry Goldman and was right next to him when he was hit with shrapnel. In later years, I often wondered about this day. There we were standing side by side and he takes the hit and not me. What force determines who gets hit? At the time I couldn't dwell on it since my only thought was to get aid for him. We never crossed paths again and I often wonder if he survived."

"Somehow our ordeal in the forest ended, and we next were assigned to assist a tank unit of the First French Army. I'm assuming we were there to protect the French in their advance but they ignored our help and moved on independently. Hence, we ended up following them rather than leading them as we were originally assigned. Unfortunately my memories are dulled on this final portion of the campaign. I know we finally left the forest and moved into some small villages in the area, Obersaasheim and Wolfgantzen to name two. The villages were deserted but we discovered many of the basements were stocked with huge wooden casks of red wine. What a bonanza for us. We filled our canteens and drank heartily. We found that heating the wine in canteen cups gave us a greater buzz. I also remember the mess crew braved the enemy fire and brought us hot meals by jeep. At this time we encountered a new noise in the air. We spotted an airplane without propellers that flew over us and dropped a bomb. This was our introduction to jet airplanes. Germany was ahead of us in this technology. It was the beginning of a new type of warfare."[53]

Don Nadeau remembers coming under fire trying to bring the chow to the troops. Don's driver wanted to abandon the jeep. Don told him that as long as it drives they were leaving in the jeep.[54]

Ted Cox remembers another airplane that they called "Bed Check Charlie". Every night when the company was settled down in Belgium and the South of France, a German plane would pass over the area several times flying low and slow. The men were under orders not to smoke and not to shoot at the plane. The plane was looking for large groups of men. That information would allow the German to fire artillery at the Americans.

The Germans also developed "Buzz Bombs". These were jet propelled rockets. The motor would sputter along. They were normally fired at London. When the rocket ran out of fuel the sputtering would stop and the rocket would fall and explode. When the engine stopped you just hoped it did not land near you.

Ray Stoddard remembers, "I am vague on how this campaign in the Colmar pocket ended but we finally were granted our rest. We were taken to a farming community and I remember the luxury of sleeping in a feather bed. Life in rural France was so different from Minnesota. I remember climbing the stairs to my bedroom and peeking in an opening in the chimney and seeing hams hanging there curing in the smoke. What an efficient use of the chimney vent! These people were our hosts and we knew we were not to sample the hams – as tempting as it was. After a few days in this village we again were loaded on the "40 & 8's" headed for Holland."[55]

The Regimental action against the enemy report for the month of February listed Capt James S. Drake as being awarded the Bronze Star.[56] This was the first of several to be awarded to Fox men during the War. The 291st had battalion and company commanders hold critiques on operations in Belgium and France.

HOLLAND, DEFENDING THE WEST SIDE OF THE MAAS RIVER
✭ ✭ ✭

*A machine gun opened up on our right flank, but the gunner
simply swept the beach, the bullets went over our heads.*

STARTING ON FEBRUARY 12TH, the 75th ID started moving back to the
north. The motor movement made about 220 miles a day, stopping in
France, then Belgium and finally Holland. On February 19th, the 291st
relieved elements of the 3rd British Parachute Brigade of the British
6th Airborne Division and occupied a defensive sector along the Maas
River.[57] Fox Company was positioned near Haelen, Holland. The town
of Haelen was located on west side of the Maas River. The Maas is called
the Meuse in France and Belgium. The Germans held the other side.
The people of Holland welcomed Fox Company. The men of Fox lived
in civilian houses. The owners stayed in their basement and the soldiers
stayed on the upper floors. The Dutch people did not have a lot of food
but they had apples growing everywhere. We gave them sugar and coffee
and they in turn made us apple fritters. LT Cox remembers every night
the family he lived with cleaned his boots.

The 291st Regimental operations overlay for February 21, 1945
showed the Regiment was on the right or south side of the 75th ID. The
Regiment deployed with 1st Battalion on the right or south, 2nd Battalion
was in the middle and 3rd Battalion on the left or north.[58]

The actions against the enemy report for February stated plans
for patrol activities were formulated several days in advance, allowing

for training of the patrol. Patrolling on the German side of the river required that the operation be planned to the minutest detail. Up to February 26th, patrols were sent out every other night across the Maas River. After that date, the Regiment sent out two patrols each night.[59]

Fox Company received 4 new officers and about 100 men which brought the company up to its authorized complement of 6 officers and 190 men. The enlisted men were a mixture of air corps men, and a number who had just finished 13 weeks of basic training. The Army had again decided it needed more infantrymen as opposed to airmen. One new arrival was Tom Taylor who had been two weeks from being made a 2LT in the Air Corps. Some men came from service support units in the rear areas of France. An article in the *Stars and Stripes*, dated January 28, 1945, stated 5,000 service support soldiers had already been reassigned to the Infantry. General Omar Bradley wrote in his book *A soldier's story*, that getting infantry replacements was a problem in Europe. Part of the problem was the large number of casualties in the Infantry. Three out of four casualties in an Infantry Division were in the rifle platoons. Another problem was that the War Department in November 1944 cut the monthly replacements to Europe from 80,000 to 67,000 men. The War Department was sending more men to the Pacific.[60]

One officer was LT Denton, an older man out of the Army Reserves Corps. LT Denton became the Company XO. Three of the officers were fresh out of Officer Candidate School (OCS), brand new 2nd LT's. 2LT Seymour was later killed on patrol across the Rhine River. 2LT Buchannan was wounded at Rutgers Castle. 2LT Stegen was wounded on the last day Fox Company was in combat.

Dick Siakel was an eighteen year old replacement arriving in Fox Company in Holland. As stated earlier in the summer of 1944, eighteen year old soldiers did not have to deploy. But after casualties mounted up in the battle for Europe, the policy was changed.[61]

An overlay dated February 20th showed how the rifle platoon positions of 2nd Battalion were positioned. Only one platoon of Fox was shown, occupying a position abreast with Company E's platoons.[62] A copy of the 291st Regimental overlay dated February 21st showed 1st, 2nd and 3rd Battalions defending along the Maas River with 2nd Battalion in the middle. 2nd Battalion defended with Companies E and F and G defending along the river. The symbols for Companies E and F are in the same company position.[63] Given these two overlays it is assumed

Company F minus one platoon was the Regimental reserve but its position was not shown.

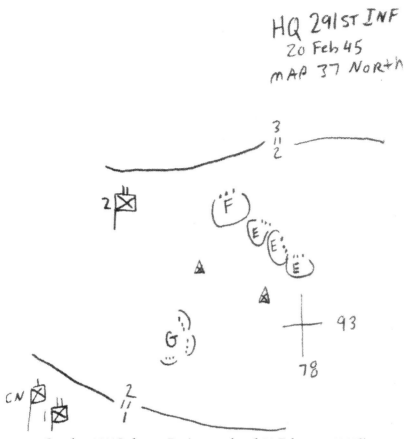

Overlay 291ˢᵗ Infantry Regiment, dated 20 February 1945[64]

Ted Cox wrote the following about LT Robert Stegen. On or about February 20ᵗʰ a good looking 20 year old 2LT, fresh out of Fort Benning OCS reported to me. His name was Robert Stegen. He gave me a snappy salute; I shook hands with him and asked if he would like to go get some hot chocolate. At the time we didn't get too friendly with new men because we may lose them very soon.

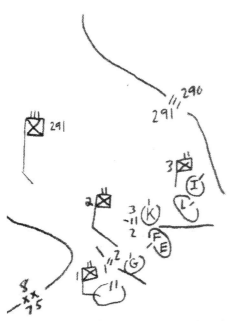

Overlay, 291st Infantry Regiment, dated 21 February 1945[65]

A brand new 2LT usually gets the first nasty job and LT Stegen was brand new and just right for the job. He got to take a combat patrol across the Maas River. His mission was to find where the German troops were located and bring back a prisoner if possible. To try to take a prisoner without firing a weapon, Stegen's men used some socks filled with sand. They practiced whacking a dummy, that looked like a German soldier, on the head and neck. They practiced until they were satisfied that if they whacked a German he certainly wouldn't make a sound.

Stegen had a couple of days to pick his men and train them in his operations plans. The night of the crossing, engineers brought forward boats that could hold 6 men, who paddled the boat across the river. Cox went down to the river and watched Stegen and his men get in their boats and begin to paddle quietly toward the other shore. Cox did not know what they would encounter on the other side of the river. Would they be spotted and machine gunned as they landed? Would they land ok, then have to fight their way back. Those thoughts knaw at a commander's stomach all the time they are gone. LT Stegen and his men returned safely with valuable information as to the disposition of German troops. The patrol could not get close to the enemy positions because the Germans had strung a wire on which they hung tin cans to serve as early warning. The patrol had to get back before sun up because at the river they had to cross a half mile of open sand bar before they would get to the cover of the trees.

Dick Forni wrote about the same patrol. "In Holland I was given eight more men (replacements) which brought the squad up to full strength. We also had a new platoon leader, LT Stegen, also a replacement. Sgt Thomas had been handling the job platoon leader, ever since LT Thompson was wounded. The day that I received the new men, we were ordered to take a recon patrol across the river, and then LT Stegen would bring the combat patrol across. I took the recon patrol across at about 9 PM, and penetrated fairly deep into enemy territory. A machine gun opened up on our right flank, but the gunner simply swept the beach area in a fan like motion, and although the gun came in our direction, the bullets went over us. We could see the gunners get out of the position and go back to their billet. We also could see guards on the road; another machine gun opened up on our left flank, but it was pointed away from us. I brought the recon patrol back to the beach and there LT Stegen had brought the combat patrol across. I took him and the patrols to where I had been, pointed out the machine positions and the guards. He took some of the men and went ahead a little ways, but came back. We had to get back to the beach before day [66]break, otherwise we would have been in plain sight of the Germans. We all made it back. The patrol was suppose to pick up a German prisoner, if we could. We didn't but I think we gave enough information about the strength of the enemy across the river to make up for our not bringing back a prisoner."

After the Colmar Pocket, Ray Stoddard was able to stay with a French family. Ray reflects on the time defending the Maas. "After leaving the comfort of the feather bed we entrained to Holland where we got new troop replacements and a Coca Cola ration (one 6 oz. bottle per man. While there, I talked with an English speaking Dutch family, whose two sons of military age hid for over two years under their chicken house to avoid conscription by the German occupiers. I have memories of a town named Bugganum where we stayed a few days and were warned about foraging in the stores and houses as they might be booby trapped. We avoided suspicious looking cash registers and drawers."

"During this time we relieved a Canadian regiment. In one of the houses, the Canadians had set up a wonderful table sand box that showed the terrain where all the opposing troops were located. Apparently the Canadians had gone across the river on patrols and returned with information that could be transferred visually into the sand. Also, I was grateful for some neat percussion grenades (tennis ball size wrapped in velvet) that they gave me and that I was able to use later on."

"My next memory is firing my '03 through a broken picture window of a house that faced down an incline towards other houses perhaps a couple hundred yards away. I pulled off a few rounds at what I perceived was movement ahead. From that position we moved to the right, and I next recall crouching behind an embankment looking for targets."[67]

Don Nadeau remembers that he set up the company kitchen in a tavern. One day, in between cooking meals, a German artillery or mortar round came through the tavern's roof. Kitchen equipment was pushed around but no cooks were in the building at that time.[68] Dick Siakel remembers that it was a close call because the company was formed up on the main road to march to the chow line.[69]

LT Cannon was transferred to take command of Easy Company. LT Foster Jones was in the 291st Infantry Regiment's Cannon Company, which does its fighting out of sight of the enemy. Jones wanted to be where the action was. So around March 1st, he was transferred to Fox to lead 2nd platoon.

DEFENDING THE WEST SIDE OF THE RHINE RIVER

✳ ✳ ✳

*The patrol launched their boat long after dark. About the
time to land, we heard burp guns and other small arms
open up. We knew then that there was trouble.*

ON MARCH 2ND THE 291st Regiment moved north under the control
of XVI Corps to an assembly area near Sustern, Holland and then
to an assembly area at Lohm, Holland. On March 3rd 291st Infantry
Regiment crossed the Maas and moved east to hold a line between
Arcen and Stadt Straelen, Germany. 2nd battalion was in the lead of
the Regiment. 2nd Battalion was renamed Task Force Drain for this
mission. Attached to Task Force Drain was a platoon from Cannon
Company, a platoon of tanks from the 772nd Tank Battalion, and a
platoon from the 275th Engineer Battalion. Task Force Drain met only
scattered enemy resistance of small arms fire, mines and road blocks.[70]
When Fox Company moved through Germany, Fred Reither saw great
destruction of towns.[71]

Now that the Division was on enemy soil, the 75th ID cautioned we
would no longer be seen as liberators but as conquerors. All civilians
were to be treated with suspicion, particularly males between the ages
of 17 to 30. Civilians had to be interrogated and suspected Nazi party
men singled out.[72]

On March 4th, 2nd Battalion was given the defensive mission of
outposting the 291st Regimental sector, while 1st and 3rd Battalions

were held in reserve. Fox Company was positioned near the village of Milchplatz. Milchplatz was east of the town of Rheinberg on the Rhine River and south of the City of Wesel.

Ted Cox writes about crossing the Maas River and moving to the Rhine River. On or about March 5th we crossed the Maas River and found ourselves on German soil. The Germans didn't put up much resistance, until we got to the Rhine River. We went part way in trucks then on foot right behind the leading assault force. Fox and 2nd Battalion mopped up where the 35th Infantry Division by passed German positions and there were several of them. Fox took some farm buildings for our CP and the troops could sleep inside. The farm buildings were along a levee and the levee was about 100 yards from the Rhine River. The Company CP was in a house with an attached barn about 200 yards from the levee.

Fox's mission was to hold our side of the river and patrol across the river to get as much information about the strength and disposition of the German troops. Once, Fox soldiers encountered a German patrol. There was a little fire fight and the next morning we found a German soldier hiding under a wagon. He could not get on the boat so he hid till he could give himself up in the morning. One night a machine gun opened up on when they saw a German boat. The next morning a dead German was lying on the beach.

Dick Siakel remembers arriving at the Rhine in total darkness. 1st squad was told it was going on patrol. They were told to be very quiet as there were Germans out patrolling. " One fellow had a reel of telephone wire that was unwinding going "EEK EEK EEK", Be quiet! Oh, yes!" [73]

The next morning, Siakel went up to the attic where S/Sgt Joe Kirk had moved one of the tiles in the tile roof and was looking out with Binoculars. "Hey Sickel, have ya ever seen the Rahinne". (Rhine with a Southern drawl) As they looked out they could see Germans marching in squad formation in the changing of the guard. Two Germans would come out of a dugout and two others go in, then they march to the next dugout. Kirk called for artillery (it took forever!). When the first shells came they hit 500 to 600 yards to the right. The Germans disappeared like prairie dogs. Shortly after this, a mortar shell hit the roof of the building. No one was hurt, just a lot of dust. Consequently 1st squad did not spend any more time in the attic.[74]

Fox received orders to send a patrol across the Rhine on the night of March 12th. LT Seymour and Sgt Brooks volunteered to take the patrol across. Other men from Fox were Sgt Calcagno, PFC Gustizia,

PFC Mora and Pvt Claussen went on the patrol. PFC Bushka and PFC Mattos and another man from 3rd Battalion headquarters went also. The night of the crossing, engineers brought forward a 12 man boat. Six men were positioned on each side of the boat to paddle across the Rhine. The patrol launched their boat long after dark. About the time they were to land, we heard burp guns and other small arms open up. We knew then that there was trouble. The boat returned and everyone on board was wounded. PFC Mora was mortally wounded. LT Seymour, Sgt Brooks and PFC Giustizia did not return. They had disembarked the boat and were on the east bank when the Germans opened up. The boat had landed 200 yards up stream. The remaining men were able bring the boat back to just below the launching point. Two days later the bodies of Seymour, Brooks, and Giustizia were found down river, dead from small arms fire. The Regimental S3 journal had an entry, at 0740 on March 13th, that 2nd Battalion reported the losses of men from Fox's patrol.[75] Again Higher Headquarters wanted Fox to do a report of Survey on the lost weapons and other equipment. Ted Cox told them that he was not doing the report on equipment lost in battle. On March 15, 1945, Ted Cox was promoted to Captain. After LT Seymour was killed, T/Sgt Irwin Chitwood accepted a battlefield promotion to 2LT, given that he could stay with 3rd platoon.

On March 12th and 14th enemy aircraft attacked the 291st sector. Anti-aircraft batteries shot down one enemy aircraft.[76] The 291st S3 journal on March 17th had an entry that an enemy aircraft dropped a bomb in the 2nd Battalion area.[77]

Cox had orders from above to move the cattle to safety away from any artillery fire that was surely to come. Thinking LT Stegen being from Utah he should be able to ride a horse and round up all the cattle between the levee and the river. LT Stegen couldn't ride a horse but had a sergeant and some men that could. He got the job done and even though it was against the rules, his platoon enjoyed eating some fresh beef.

Dick Forni writes about defending the Rhine River. "We did guard duty on the beach at night. I took half the squad out one night and Sgt Wallace took the other half the next night. [78] In addition to defending the west bank of the Rhine, companies of the 291st were involved in Military Government work, screening civilians and evacuating suspected Nazis.

When Fox arrived at the Rhine, British General Montgomery gave orders that we were not to fire at the Germans across the river, because we had to conserve all our ammo. We had to watch the Germans digging in on the other side of the river. LT Jones and some other guys found a small cannon that the Germans had left behind. They manhandled it to the top of the levee, loaded and fired one round at the Germans on the other side. That was a gesture of our determination to do them harm. Don't think it bothered the Germans too much. The Germans had a big gun mounted on a railroad base. Don't know caliber it was but it fired a shell for miles. You could hear the gun firing long before you heard the shell rustling overhead.

Dick Siakel remembers German search lights on the Rhine River. "Every night Fox would go to the river bank and dig in. One night the company went as far as the hedge row and planted ourselves down. Some time later four search lights flashed across the river for about 30 second. Needless to say, we buried our faces. The next night the company stopped at the same hedgerow. Immediately, at least a dozen lights lit up the entire area for about 30 seconds. Were they thinking we were going to cross the river? Or were they wondering about all those holes Fox dug along the river bank?"[79]

Ray Stoddard remembers the Rhine River. "Once we made it to the Rhine River we were billeted in various houses well behind the Rhine embankment. Under cover of darkness we holed up in a farm house within sight of the opposite shoreline. We went in there at night and stayed until the next evening as we would have been exposed during the day to the opposing forces. Once in the farm house we bedded down in the basement. I remember going out during daylight and lying behind the shoreline embankment seeking and zeroing in on moving targets three hundred yards or so across the river. I was most intrigued by the constant drone of Piper Cub airplanes cruising slowly above us spotting targets for their artillery. We continued tracking between our billets and the farm house for several days. New replacements joined us while there and they were selected to accompany Sgt. Brooks on a night patrol crossing. They had barely reached the opposite shore when they met resistance. Sgt. Brooks never made it back but was finally found later floating in the river near Amsterdam. For two of the replacements this "baptism under fire" hit them emotionally; they didn't stay long with us."[80]

1LT John Affeldt on the left with PFC Joe Affeldt on March 23, 1945

Joe Affeldt had an older brother John, who commanded Headquarters Company in 3rd Battalion 314th Infantry Regiment of the 79th ID. The details are not remembered but Joe and John ran into each other during the Battle of the Bulge, probably after January 25th 1945, when Fox had attacked south. On March 23rd, the day before the 79th ID would the assault across the Rhine River, Joe and John met in the town of Rheinberg, west of the Fox defensive position.[81]

During the month of March 2LT Irwin Chitwood was awarded the Bronze Star.[82]

CROSSING THE RHINE RIVER

All Hell broke loose. Fifty five battalions of artillery
and all the division's mortars opened up

TED COX REMEMBERS THAT on March 24th at 2 AM we woke up to a barrage of 55 battalions of artillery plus all the mortars in the Division. They poured fire on the German positions on the east side of the river. The pounding continued for one hour. Counterfire from the Germans hit our CP and a 4.2 inch Mortar emplacement behind the CP. Two mortar men were killed and two wounded. The seats of their jeep caught fire and Fox men quickly put out the fire. Cox decided if someone can steal the Fox mess trailer we now had the chance to get a third jeep. The jeep was hidden behind a dairy barn. When the German artillery round hit the Company CP. Cox was lifted off his feet and thrown 8 to 10 feet. The house the CP was in had a stone fireplace. The fireplace was nothing but a pile of bricks and stones. Beryl Lantz had been on duty on the Rhine River bank. He returned to the Company CP to get some sleep in a corner of the basement. A short time later he was rudely awakened when the house collapsed into the basement. Lantz did not get a scratch. LT Denton was billeted about a half mile away. When LT Denton first saw the CP, he thought he had inherited the job of company commander.

The 75th ID was part of XVI Corps. When it was time for XVI Corps to cross the Rhine River the 79th ID crossed first followed by the 35th ID in assault boats. Pontoon bridges were put in to allow the supply trucks of the 79th and 35th ID to cross.

At 3:05 am the attack across the Rhine started. Elements of the 79th ID passed through the 291st Regiment sector to cross the river. At daylight Fox could see Navy landing craft lined up bumper to bumper on the road that went across the levee. The landing craft was used to transport assault troops and tanks across the Rhine. The pontoon bridge was almost completed on March 24th. But one Navy landing craft lost power and drifted into the bridge. The damage was so bad the engineers had to take it apart and start all over again. On March 25th the bridge was completed, all the while under artillery fire from the Germans. A direct hit was made on one of the boats killing 3 engineers. The pontoon bridges were put in to allow the follow on units and the supply trucks of the 79th ID. After the 79th the 35th ID crossed the river.

Ray Stoddard remembers the following about crossing the Rhine River. "The time came for troops to cross the river. We were in reserve and our company was stretched out in foxholes on top of the embankment. My hole was really deep due to sandy soil and easy digging. Also I had topped my hole with scrap wood so I was well covered. That night is forever in my memory. It was all flashes of light and constant booming of the artillery rounds going overhead and even some short rounds landing close to our positions. It was grossly noisy and eerie and during all this I could catch glimpses of the engineers down on the river bank trying to push a pontoon bridge out on the river under intense fire. Later, I heard that their first attempt had been unsuccessful as one of the bridge sections suffered a direct hit and collapsed. But they finally got the job done and the next day we watched what looked like our whole Army on wheels and treads rolling across that bridge. During all the crossing fireworks, a Chemical Mortar unit had set up in front of my home billet. A chemical mortar fired a white phosphorus round to create a smoke screen. They had drawn enemy fire and the house I had called home was no more. It had gone up in flames. My personal stuff was stashed there and I lost it all. I had quite an attachment to a nicely sized canvass bag that I had scrounged from a British unit. It was an elongated bag that had a wooden stick attached to stiffen it, and I had fashioned a buckle for it to fit on the back of my ammo belt. It was just large enough to hold a couple K rations boxes and some other items and fit very nicely into the small of my back. My prized invention burned up when the house was destroyed."

"We stayed at that crossing for several days guarding the bridge. We were supplied with a new sub machine gun (M10) which we nicknamed the "grease gun." This weapon was useful for shooting detritus floating in the water. Even General Eisenhower and Prime Minister Churchill visited the bridge. I had walked back from the river a distance and was thunderstruck at the sight of the big artillery guns emplaced to protect the crossing. I had never seen so much massive artillery placed hub to hub. Even the Navy was there with their boats on trailers ready for the Rhine crossing."[83]

Left to Right LT Buchannan, LT Jones, Capt Cox, LT Stegen at the Rhine River. The pontoon bridge is in the background.

3rd Battalion 291st guarded bridges named George and Howe. 1st Battalion guarded bridge Love. 2nd Battalion patrolled between the bridges Love and Nan. The 291st Regimental overlay dated March 26th showed Company G was given the mission of guarding Bridge Nan, positioning platoons on both sides of the bridge. Company F patrolled from bridge Nan to halfway to bridge Love.

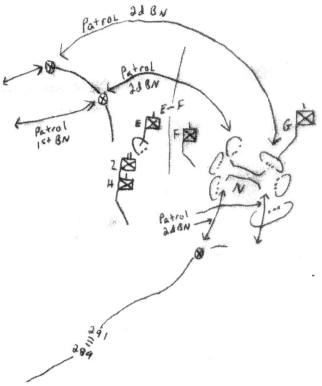

Overlay, 291ˢᵗ Infantry Regiment, dated 26 March 1945[84]

The mission of the 291ˢᵗ Infantry Regiment was to hold these bridges at all cost. German aircraft were active in the 291ˢᵗ Regiment sector. Several bombs were dropped in 3ʳᵈ Battalion's sector. Anti-aircraft batteries reported shooting down one German plane in the 291ˢᵗ sector.[85]

The British put up large barrage balloons at each end of the bridges and about 50 yards apart from the ends of the bridges. Every night a German plane would fly over. The British antiaircraft guns would open up. The next morning the bridge was still intact but the balloons were all shot down. The British would put them up again and when night came the same thing happened. Three nights we were there, the British would put up their balloons in the daytime and shoot them down at night. The British were resolute though. They never shot down a plane but they sure shot their balloons down and put them back up.

March 25, 1945, German POW's double timing across the Rhine River.

Every night we would watch the British air force bomb cities in the Ruhr, such as Essen and Dortmund. There was real fireworks every night. The spotlights would sweep the sky. The ack ack would be bursting in the air. When a bomber got hit it would provide another light in the sky. On March 23rd we watch the American Air Corps, A-20 Havoc's bomb the City of Wesel, without any anti air craft fire opposing them.

Ted Cox continues about the time on the Rhine River. Stegen and I decided to reconnoiter the other side of the river using the new bridge the engineers built. On the far side we found a shed full of boats, some had been damaged by artillery. One little kayak looked so good I told Bob we should paddle it back across the river. I planned to dismantle the kayak and ship it home. We started across and the current was carrying us downriver toward the bridge. We had forgotten that we had given our troops, who were guarding the bridge, orders to shoot anything that floats. We paddled as hard as we could and finally got to shore. An enlisted man came running from the bridge and proceeded to chew us out. He said we were lucky they didn't shoot us. We went back to our quarters thanking our lucky stars that we were still alive.

THE BATTLE FOR THE RUHR

★ ★ ★

*Lt Stegen looked out the back door and did not see any
Germans out there so he slipped out the back door. Just as he
turned to the right, a German came around the corner.*

THE OBJECTIVE OF ALLIED forces was the destruction of the German
Army in the Ruhr Area. The Ruhr was the most heavily industrialized
section of Germany, and perhaps even Europe at the time. The loss of
the Ruhr meant any chance of continued German resistance would fade
almost immediately. Within the Ruhr were many defensible obstacles
for the German Army to use, from heavily forested areas, canals, to
industrial complexes that housed snipers. The 75th ID would advance
into this region attached to the Ninth Army's XVI Corps. This would
be an operation primarily for the foot soldiers of the attacking infantry
divisions, but not without close artillery, air, and tank/tank destroyer
support. Facing the 75th during this drive stood elements of the German
116th Panzer Division, 180th, 190th and 2nd Parachute Divisions.[86]

On March 28th , the 291st crossed the Rhine River's pontoon bridge
by truck convoy, assembling vicinity Mollen Germany. Fox and the
75th ID was under the control of the 9th Army, commanded by General
Simpson. The 75th ID was on the right flank of the 9th Army and Fox was
the right flank of the 75th ID.

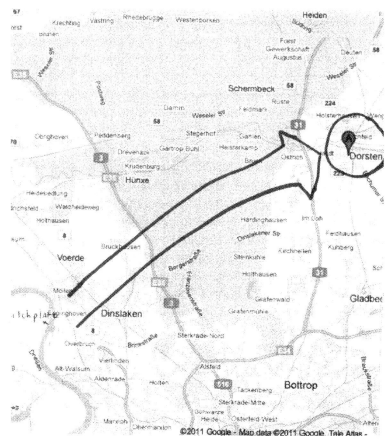

Google Map of Dorsten, Germany[87]

Fox closed on Dorsten where we relieved elements of the 79th ID. On March 29th at 0700 after a brief artillery barrage we attacked the town of Marl. The Germans did not have much fight left in them and they surrendered in bunches. 2nd Battalion captured intact a large synthetic rubber plant at Huls. The plant used slave labors. So we captured a slave labor camp and released the laborers, which were mostly Russian and Italians, 3,000 persons were liberated from two camps. One of the laborers, Jose Lopez, tells the conditions at the camp. This validates the need to destroy the Nazis Regime. This quote comes from the pamphlet titled "The 75th Division in Combat" produced by the G3 section right after the war at Camp Baltimore. Lopez was from southern Spain and was probably caught in France and forced to do labor for the Germans.

"I am from Andalusia. I have been working at this factory for 25 months. Before that I was working in France. I was told that I would be paid 20 Marks a month for myself for working at the factory and that the main part of my salary would be sent to my family in France. They are poor people and need the money. But I have received letters from my family and they have not received any money. I was very poorly fed and worked very hard. I worked 12 hours a day, shoveling cement. Since I came to the factory I have lost 15 kilos and have suffered much from the cold. I have rheumatism so badly that I can only walk with great difficulty. Also I have contracted tuberculosis. If any of the laborers refused to work they were locked up and given no food. The next day they were willing to work."[88]

2nd Battalion continued to attack east to the town of Sickingmuhle. On March 30th after a brief artillery barrage, 2nd Battalion attacked. Fox Company was supposed to take the south part of town and G Company was to take the north end of town. We took our part of town without much resistance. But G Company was held up at a small creek about a half mile out of town by small arms fire.

In case some Germans soldiers were in the open, Cox had machine guns fire a few bursts. As Fox Company advanced they passed a house, which the men searched. A German woman was the only occupant and was dead, killed by the machine gun fire. Cox hated that she was killed by his orders and he thought of her many times after the war. But that is one of those things that happen in war.

LT Stegen's 1st platoon was chasing Germans and wound up in Company G's sector. He encountered a large force of Germans and his platoon took cover in a large house. He left half his platoon to hold the bottom floor the rest went upstairs. On the second floor, his men found a German officer, who wanted to surrender. One of his men wanted to shoot the officer but LT Stegen ordered that the German not be harmed. The Germans had an antitank weapon called a panzerfaust and they were firing this weapon at the brick tiles on the roof of the house. The explosions from the panzerfausts showered the men on the second floor with bits of tile.[89]

Stegen used his SCR 600 to radio his location and problem, but he could not send from inside the room. He would poke the radio antennae outside the window just long enough to send his message. Then the Germans would begin firing at him and he would pull back into the room. Cox could hear enough to know he was in trouble and Cox could hear the firing. Stegen tried the second time and Cox got his location. S/Sgt Adams was standing nearby and Cox took him and they double timed toward the shooting. We got within a block of the racket. Cox saw an open window to a house. He dived through the window with Adams right behind him. They saw an old man in his bed looking at them with a pitiful stare. He looked to be about 90 years old and looked as I he was dying. When he saw two armed American soldiers come through his window, he probably thought he would be shot.

They did not hesitate a minute there and went to the front door. There S/Sgt Adams gave Cox a direct order. He said:" Cap'n you stay here." Cox stayed there while Adams went toward Stegen's house, firing his rifle as he ran. Cox thought Adams was going to take on a large enemy force single handed. But just then a squad of Fox's riflemen showed up and joined in the action, causing the Germans to retreat. The Germans probably retreated when they received accurate fire from a different direction. For his actions Adams received a Bronze Star.

LT Stegen told this story about the engagement. He looked out the back door and did not see any Germans out there so he slipped out the door. Just as he turned to his right, a German came around the corner. Stegen had his carbine with an anti-tank grenade mounted. But the pin was not pulled. Both Stegen and the German were surprised. Stegen fired his carbine hitting the German soldier in the shoulder with the rifle grenade, knocking him down. The German got up and ran back around the corner. Stegen ran back into the house. Both of them must have considered themselves lucky.

Cox called Company G on the SCR 300 radio and told them Fox had secured their sector of Sickingmuhle and found they were still trying to get across a creek. They were still held up by machine gun fire. About dark, Company G made it to Sickingmuhle.

Later, LT Stegen found a badly wounded German soldier. Suddenly a bunch of German women came out of a bomb shelter. LT Stegen gestured to the women to take care of the wounded soldier. Soon after this happened another German soldier stood up from his near by hiding place and threw down his rifle. The question that can not be known is what would have happened if Stegen had not obtained aid for the wounded German. Would the other soldier have fired his weapon instead of surrendering? [90]

The Regimental overlay for March 31st showed 2nd Battalion on the left/north and 3rd Battalion on the right/south. 1st Battalion was in the rear located with the 291st Regiment Command post. The 289th Regiment was on the right/south of the 291st. Another Division was to the left/north of the 291st Regiment. This overlay showed the position of 2nd Battalion units after the attack on Sickingmuhle. Companies E, F and G are closely located, probably around the town of Sickingmuhle. The 2nd Battalion CP was located near Fox.

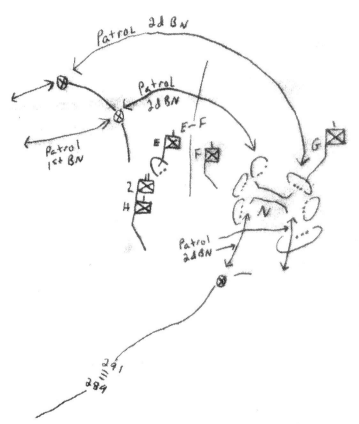

Overlay 291st Infantry Regiment, dated 31 March 1945[91]

On March 31st, Fox continued on toward Datteln, riding tanks through the Die Haard Forest. Stegen had a tank platoon of 5 tanks attached to his platoon. Before going to Officer Candidate School for the Infantry, Bob Stegen had made sergeant and tank commander in the 16th Armored Division. Die Haard forest was a managed forest, with wide spaces between trees. Stegen with his infantry and attached tank platoon went up and down the forest but did not find any Germans. At dusk Stegen came to a large chateau. The front doors were 12 feet tall. When Stegen entered he found a large family of 20 to 30 people at a large table. A German officer in a black uniform stood up. The German said he wanted to surrender and asked that his family not be harmed. When asked if he had any weapons he showed Stegen a large collection of hunting weapons. He gave Stegen a fancy black scabbard belt. Stegen did not want to carry it so he gave it to one of his soldiers. Stegen left two soldiers to guard the house until Company E moved up.[92]

Fox was going through a village when Cpl Coleman stopped the headquarters group by a house where the family was just sitting down to dinner. Coleman rousted them out and the headquarters group sat down to a sumptuous meal of roast beef, roast pork, mashed potatoes, fresh cooked vegetables and home made bread. While we were enjoying our meal, a little old lady knocked on the door and asked if she could have some milk for her baby. Cox said she could have some and Coleman gave her a small glass of milk. On April 1st we were still hot on the heels of the fleeing Germans. We moved into the outskirts of Datteln where we set up defensive positions at the junction of the Lippe and Dortmund Erns canals. From the time we left Dorsten we had been moving eastward with the Lippe canal on our left.

In the Pacific on April 1, 1945, US forces invaded Okinawa and it took till June 21, 1945 to control the island. Over 100,000 Japanese soldiers were killed or captured and tens of thousands local civilians were killed, wounded or committed suicide. There were more than 62,000 American casualties. This led to fears that invading the Japanese main land would result in a million American casualties.[93]

Fox stayed in Datteln about 3 days where they got some well earned rest. Fox took a nice hotel for our headquarters. Some of the men stayed in rooms of the hotel while others took over some nice homes. We treated the civilians very nice but we took what we wanted from them. To the victor go the spoils of war was our motto.

When we entered the hotel, all the employees were on duty. They just watched as Sgt Nadeau had his men drag the kitchen equipment over the nicely polished hardwood floors of the Hotel Datteln. We only owned and managed it for 3 days, then we left town, never to return again.

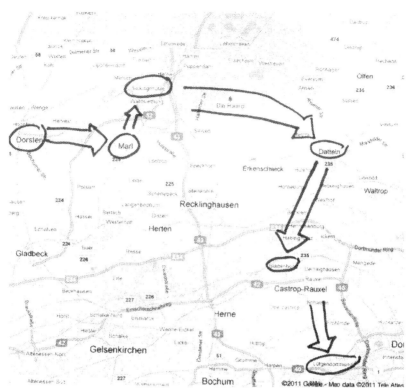

Google Map of Castrop-Rauxel, Germany[94]
*Fox Company path of attack from Dorsten east to Marl. Next Fox
attack northeast to Sickingmuhle. From Sickingmuhle, Fox cleared
the Die Haard Forest to the east. Then Fox attacked south to Datteln.
From Datteln Fox attacked South to Castrop-Rauxel and then
Lutgendortmund. Lutgendortmund is in the southeast corner of the map.*

LTC Drain reconnoitered a canal crossing by walking over a blown bridge. On April 4th, the 291st crossed the canal at 0100 exploiting a small bridgehead. Fred Reither remembers going on a 10 man patrol to determine if a bridge was still standing. Near their objective, Reither and three others stayed at a position while the others went forward to observe the bridge, which they found the Germans were still using.[95]

Fox like other Infantry Companies was capturing many Germans. Ed Letourneau remembers the Germans would throw their weapons on the ground and walk towards Fox with their hands in the air. A few soldiers would be detailed to guard the German prisoners as they walked to the rear. Behind the lines of Fox, these prisoners would be turned over to other units who took the prisoners further back. Finally miles to the rear the prisoners would be placed in holding areas.

Military historians often write about the fog of war. The fog of war includes the uncertainty during war of knowing the enemies capabilities, positions and intentions. Red Carr told a humorous story about 3rd Squad, 2nd Platoon going on a night patrol in Germany. During the patrol, the squad heard metal on metal sounds to their front. The squad took cover in a ditch while trying to understand the enemy situation. The metal on metal sounds continued through the night and moved around. At daylight, the squad found they were on the edge of a pasture with horses wearing bells.[96]

Fox got orders from Battalion headquarters to attack anywhere we could find Germans. So we moved southward toward the industrial area of Dortmund. The Germans were masters at fighting delaying actions. They would dig in a small group with machine guns and panzerfausts. When we got in range they would begin firing on Fox. We would naturally go to ground and begin the process of working around to get in position to storm their defensive position. Sometimes that might take several hours. When we assaulted their position we would often find an empty machine gun nest. The Germans had done their job of giving their main body several hours to prepare a defensive position or gain more time to move on.

S/Sgt Earl Adams told his son a story about how luck was a factor to keep you alive in combat. Adams' squad was to maneuver around a machine gun position and attack it from the flank. But the Germans saw them and repositioned their machine gun. Adams had his men in an assault position and stood up to lead the attack. He took one step and slipped in the mud and fell flat on his face just as the machine gun let off a burst. His squad ran past him yelling "You killed my sergeant" and took out the machine gun.

The Regimental after-action report for April 1945 stated the following, "In Datteln the 291st found three huge steel and concrete air raid bunkers designed to withstand blockbuster bombs. The shelters were built to accommodate the city's entire population 27,000 people. The bunkers resembling huge barns covered an area of 150,000 square feet. There were two stories above ground and one story below ground. The walls and sharply slanted roofs were of reinforced concrete six to eight feet thick. The bunkers were equipped with central heating units, sewage and ventilation systems, running water and electricity. However the utilities were knocked out by the retreating Wehrmacht demolition squads. Evidence that they could withstand terrific punishment were the flattened buildings surrounding them."[97]

On April 6th at 0500 Cox met LTC Drain to get orders for the day. Fox was to continue east with a canal on our right until we reached a road that ran south toward Castrop-Rauxel. We were to straddle the road and move to the next phase line where we had to stop and wait for further orders. Our phase line was a railroad line and a canal side by side that ran east and west. This was about 3 miles north of the town of Castrop-Rauxel. The rail line and canal showed on the map but the map did not show any buildings.

Companies F and G would lead the attack with Company E in reserve. Fox moved out and the only resistance we had was one rifleman. He would fire two or three shots and run. We had two tank destroyers supporting us. After we had advanced about a mile south we came upon a large castle, setting on the left side of the road.

Cox does not know why it was called Rutgers castle since there was not a town of Rutgers near by. But to the east of the Castle is a Chemical plant called Rutgers with ¨over the u. A Google map search did not show any castles in the industrial park. Stegen remembers his military map had the castle identified as Rutgers. The 291st Infantry Regiment's history states the Regimental headquarters from April 7th through the 9th was at Rutgers Castle.

This history will use Rutgers as the name of the Castle, since that is the name Fox men knew. Research in 2011 of Google maps of the Castrop-Rauxel area, shows a Schloss Bladenhorst. Schloss is German for castle. Photos of Bladenhorst from the internet were sent to Ted Cox who confirmed that it looked like the castle known as Rutgers by Fox men.

Below the red balloon at the top left is Schloss Bladenhorst. This castle was known as Rutgers by Fox men. To the east of the castle, is Rutgers Chemical, which may be how the name Rutgers was attached to the castle.

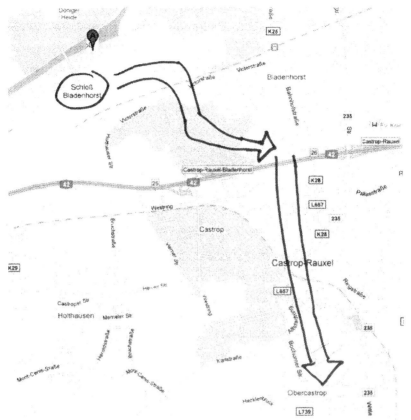

Google Map of Castrop-Rauxel with Schloss Bladenhorst, Germany[98]

Any Fox Company men who read the 291ˢᵗ Infantry Regimental history can tell you there is lots of credit given to other units that should be given to Fox Company. We know what we did and where we did it. We do not need the publicity. The men that gave their lives accomplishing these things will never know the difference.

Fox was attacking south with 1ˢᵗ and 3ʳᵈ platoons. 2ⁿᵈ platoon was in reserve. We had two tank destroyers but they did not arrive until the battle was over. The Germans were dug in foxholes and bunkers on the ground in front of the castle. 1ˢᵗ and 3ʳᵈ platoons hit them with grenades and small arms fire.

S/Sgt Joseph Kirk and S/Sgt Elmer Prestridge were awarded Bronze Stars for charging across an open field under heavy enemy fire on April 6th. Kirk and Prestridge crept up to an enemy position and captured 6 German soldiers. Their awards and actions were announced in the May 18ᵗʰ issue of the *Mule* the 75ᵗʰ Infantry Division newspaper. Kirk was wounded in the fight at the castle and Nathan Henn took over as squad leader 1st squad, 2nd platoon.

Cox and LTs Buchanan and Stegen were together watching a stream of machine gun bullets ricocheting off the far wall. An artillery shell landed in the middle of the courtyard. They did not think anyone was hit until 30 minutes later Cox saw blood seeping from a small hole in Buchanan's boot. Buchanan didn't think it was serious enough to merit calling an aid man. 30 minutes later his leg started to swell and stiffening up. He was evacuated to a field hospital and never returned to Fox.

LT Foster Jones of 2nd platoon was up front since he liked to be where the action was. There was a little shack, something like a security shack back home. LT Jones had just gotten into the shack when a German, 8 feet away in a foxhole, threw a potato masher hand grenade into the open door of the shack. Jones promptly threw it back. It exploded harmlessly outside the foxhole. The German threw another grenade. Jones threw it back. The third time the German bobbed up to throw his grenade, Jones was waiting for him. Jones shot him in the head with his carbine and the German died halfway out of his hole.

After the battle there were 4 dead Germans and we took 22 men and 4 women that surrendered. At the end of the fire fight we did not have a casualty.

Cox was talking to Jones by the lead M10 tank destroyer, the TD commander was standing in his open turret, with half his body showing above the vehicle, when he fell over dead. He was shot by a sniper off to the east.

Fox had reached it's phase line, which was the canal, and we were ready to move on. But when Cox called battalion headquarters, the radio did not work. We had orders not to pass the phase line until we got orders. It was assumed Battalion had to coordinate with other units.

Here we were fresh from a successful fight and eager to get on with the next one. Cox moved to the bank of the canal and about 200 yards away in the road, Cox saw a tank obstacle. A German would pop out from behind this obstacle and wave a black flag. All of us thought he wanted to surrender. We yelled at him, "kamerad". We waved at him to come in. He would wave the black flag and then disappear behind the obstacle. Several times he did this and we would continue to yell for him to come on in.

Suddenly there was a tremendous explosion. The first thing Cox thought was that a German 88 or tank had fired and that the shell had hit right in front of him. Cox did not wait for a second shot. He ran about 20 feet behind the canal bank and jumped into a tank emplacement.

The Germans had dug in several emplacements facing west. The emplacements were dug so that a tank could fire while protected from frontal attack.

Cox's run only took a few seconds and by that time he knew what had happened. Cox was hugging the wall of the emplacement with chunks of concrete falling all around him. There was a bridge over the canal and the road across the bridge ran on to the obstacle. It was another 100 yards to the forest and then on to the town of Castrop-Rauxel, which was our objective. One of the tank destroyer commanders had said he wanted to barrel on full speed. If Fox had not had the orders to hold at the phase line, Cox might have agreed with him. The German had blown the bridge. He was trying to coax us on to the bridge by waving his black flag. Luckily no one was hurt by the falling concrete. By the time the smoke cleared the German soldier had disappeared into the woods behind him. We knew we would have to deal with him later.

Sgt Ed Neville remembers staying in a bunker waiting to move on. "Sgt Gerald Dickinson was posted as a look out. After a while Neville went to relieve Dickinson. Neville saw a German head come up on the horizon, so he stood up with his arms and shoulders out of the bunker ready to shoot. Dickinson stood with just his head over the top of the bunker. Suddenly Dickinson fell over backwards with a bullet to the head. He was dead before he hit the ground. Neville truly believed the only reason he was on this earth today is that a German could not shoot straight. Neville was a much bigger target than Gerald was."[99]

Cox could not contact Battalion Headquarters so Fox had to sit there and wait while things started unraveling. The Germans started pounding Fox with Artillery. It seemed the Germans were getting ready to counterattack, so Cox called in the second platoon which had been in reserve. Cox then decided since he was out of contact with battalion he would call Capt Cannon, commander of Easy Company to join us in case of a counterattack. Cannon had formerly lead 2nd platoon of Fox.

Cox estimated that the Germans had about 50-60 men in the attacking force. The Germans were coming out of the woods south of the castle. They had a small amount of artillery, maybe one or two guns plus mortar support. Cox would not call the German artillery a barrage.

But the Germans were landing more and more artillery rounds on the Fox positions.

LT Stegen had his 1st platoon behind the railroad tracks and they did not see the Germans until they were coming over the tracks. They were firing panzerfausts. The panzerfaust was originally developed for used against tanks. Its warhead would burn through armor similar to our bazooka. Against personnel it was just an oversized potato masher hand grenade. A soldier could carry three of them and still carry his rifle.

A Fox and Easy Companies were still out of contact with battalion. Casualties were mounting and Cox got word Dickinson was dead. Soon all of Fox and Easy Companies were engaging the Germans.

An American jeep flying a large flag with a white back ground and a big Red Cross, came to start evacuating the wounded. At Cox's request they also brought in a load of ammunition.

S/Sgt Joe Kirk, PFC Carey West and PFC Dick Siakel of second platoon took cover behind a four foot high stone wall. An artillery round hit near Carey West. A piece of shrapnel buried itself in his left lung near his heart. He was evacuated by the red cross medic jeep just before dark. His stretcher was strapped across the back of the jeep. The driver turned the corner heading north when an artillery round landed by the side of the jeep, puncturing a rear tire. A piece of shrapnel hit West in the shoulder, making him a twice wounded soldier the same day. But he could only be awarded one Purple Heart. The same round that hit West got Kirk in the legs. He had multiple shrapnel wounds in both legs. Siakel was lucky. He came through unscathed.

Years later at one of the Fox reunions, West joked with Cox that because Cox had the red cross jeep bring in ammunition and that was against the Geneva rules of warfare, the Germans were shooting at the jeep. It was a random shot. Lucky for the Germans, unlucky for West.

Bill Hayes remembers S/Sgt Jack McKay was putting men into position and a mortar or artillery round landed very close by. Jack was thrown off his feet. Hays and Reither feared the worst for Jack. But on close inspection, he only sustained a huge red splotch on his leg. McKay had a k ration can in his pocket where the fragment of the shell hit, imbedding itself in the can.[100]

Stegen saw a two Germans getting ready to fire a panzerfaust. Stegen shot one man and the other ran for cover. Stegen had a bullet pop right by his head so he moved to better cover. Later Stegen tried to go under the rail road tracks by going through an under pass that had several inches of chemicals. The chemicals got into his boots and took the skin off his feet.[101]

Cox was standing behind a short wall in front of the castle with LT Jones, Capt Cannon and the artillery forward observer (FO). Earlier one of our spotter planes was flying in the area, directing fire on targets off to the east. But the plane left just when we needed him.

The Germans were coming across the railroad tracks. Cox told the FO to call for fire 200 yards away which would have put it just over the Germans. The FO said it was too close, that if a round fell short it might hit us. Cox told him that would be a chance he would take. Cox had to give the FO a direct order to call in the fire. The FO called in one round to see where it would land. Satisfied with the one round the FO called for fire for effect. In a moment a battalion of artillery rounds exploded over the German's heads. The artillery was firing rounds with fuses developed by the British that caused the rounds to explode about 20 feet above the ground spraying shrapnel on anybody or anything that was below.

Cox told Cannon and Jones to grab some men and as soon as the artillery stopped to head across the railroad track and mop up the rest of the Germans. The two officers did not wait for their men. They charged across the open field and killed the ones that survived the artillery. They were awarded the Silver Star for their action. Cannon later told Cox that as he was running across the field he was passing a badly wounded German. The German pointed to Cannon's pistol and then to his head. Cannon obliged by shooting him in the head. Germans captured during the fighting confirmed Fox Company had been attacked by soldiers from the 2nd Parachute Division. For his actions in commanding Fox Company during the battle at the castle, Ted Cox was awarded a Bronze Star for Valor. Cox's citation read, "When out of contact with battalion headquarters Captain Cox used his own imitative in organizing Companies E and F to stop a German counterattack, resulting in many German casualties".

At Rutgers Castle PFC's Odell Barbee, Edmund Bonaldi and Charles Curtis were killed by either mortar or artillery fire. PFC Gerald Dickinson as stated earlier was killed by sniper fire. Fox Company also had eighteen men wounded on April 6th, including two lieutenants and three staff sergeants. Some men were wounded more than once.[102]

Fox men with a King Tiger tank.

After the counterattack was broken up, a runner came from Battalion headquarters requesting that Cox come to Battalion. Cpl Coleman came with him and they had to walk 3 to 4 miles west along the railroad tracks to a small village. The Battalion headquarters was upstairs in a large building. Cox was greeted by LTC Drain. Immediately the Major, who commanded the Field Artillery Battalion that supported Fox, said he was recommending the FO for a Silver Star. He said it sounded over the radio like the FO was calling in fire on his position to break up the counterattack. Cox told the Major he would demote the FO because he was too scared to call for fire 200 yards away. Cox told the Major that he had to give the FO a direct order to call for the artillery fire. Cox said the artillery gunners should be the ones getting medals because they were so accurate. Cox was angry but kept his cool. LTC Drain gave him his orders for the 7th of April to continue the attack to the South.

At 5:30 am on April 7th the Regiment continued to attack south towards Castrop-Rauxel. 1st Battalion was on the left (west) and 2nd Battalion on the right with 3rd Battalion in reserve. When Fox went on the attack on April 7th they found behind the tank obstacle the box and plunger used by the German soldier to blow up the bridge.

When Fox got to the woods, they met resistance in the form of small arms fire. The Germans were using wooden bullets which led us to believe they were running short on ammunition. The wooden bullets would fly through the air making a whirring sound. Evidently they were not rifling. But they were effective to a point. PFC Carl Randa was killed by small arms the day after Rutgers Castle while attacking through the woods and up a hill. He could have been killed by wooden bullets.

LT Thompson had returned to Fox and took over 3rd platoon. LT Chitwood was away. Chitwood had been sent to 75th ID headquarters to demonstrate how to use German weapons. A panzerfaust exploded in his hands. So he was recuperating in a hospital for a few days. LT Thompson caught a wooden bullet in his left arm, causing a terrible wound. He was evacuated and never returned to the company. Sam Drake saw him after the war, when Thompson was living in Arizona. Thompson's arm was useless, just dangling from the shoulder. Letters after the war to the Arizona address came back marked "unknown".

After we finished clearing the woods and got to a hill overlooking the town, on orders from the Battalion we stopped for the day. The Regimental Headquarters called that Col Robertson was going to pay us a visit and wanted to know what was going on. Cox told them there was just an occasional sniper fire. The Colonel never came to see us

Fox got to a hill overlooking Castrop-Rauxel and could not see any enemy activity. Cox wanted to see the effect of artillery on the tile roofs. We heard the rounds go over head. When they hit the yellow tile roofs, yellow and orange dust would fly in the air.

On April 8th, a Major from Regiment drove into town, thinking it was cleared. He came under small arms fire. The Major bailed out of the jeep and took cover in a house close by. He left his map and some important papers in his jeep. He stayed in the house until almost dark when he dressed in women's clothes and walked back unharmed. Battalion called Fox and had them send out a patrol to retrieve the papers. The patrol without opposition drove the jeep back and returned the jeep and papers to the Major.

During darkness Company G of 2nd Battalion was in advance of 2nd Battalion and got cut off by infiltrating enemy infantrymen. But pressure by Fox and Easy companies caused the enemy to withdraw and contact was resumed with George Company. The rest of the Regiment continued to clear Castrop-Rauxel on April 8th.

The Regiment defended its position south of Castrop-Rauxel on April 9th and 10th. 2nd Battalion had to fight off several counterattacks.

Ray Stoddard remembers the following about the last days of combat.

"Castrop-Rauxel is a town located in the Ruhr Valley somewhere near Dortmond. Often we had no idea where we were, but I have memory of this town because of a signpost bearing this name that I saw during fighting. What I recall in particular, after moving through woods in a skirmish line, was a bomb crater made from either a target miss or indiscriminate jettison of bombs which seemed to happen often by our Air Corps. I held up in the protection of this big hole, crouching at almost ground level on the upper edge, occupied with the reloading of my Springfield rifle. I was having trouble breaking the clip that holds the cartridges. The 1903 with scope had to be loaded singly as there was no room under the scope to push the full clip. My very cold and numb fingers were not cooperating very well in breaking out each individual round, and while doing this very awkward process, I heard running steps approaching me from the woods ahead. There were a few grey overcoated German soldiers veering off through the forest trying for a flanking movement against us. I was the last one on the right of our line as far as I was aware. I thought, "Now what to do?" My weapon was empty and somehow I had to stop these troops closing in on my hidden position. So, I tossed a grenade and ducked down when it exploded. It did the trick! The "Germans" were down and not moving. I was not going to hang around to see if there were more. There wasn't time to reload my rifle and I don't know if I had the composure to even try so I moved off to my left until I had contact with others in my squad. Once in contact with them, I remember railroad tracks and empty boxcars. On my side of the line of boxcars there was an empty industrial building. It was three stories high and had an entrance tall enough to drive a locomotive in. Inside was an overhead hoist system suspended from the ceiling. On one of the walls there was a dangling metal stairway that ascended to a metal platform at an open window. I climbed the stairway to the platform and looked out the opening. It was high enough to see over the boxcars the activity on the other side. It looked like a whole company of German troops lined up to eat. They were all clustered around a horse drawn food wagon. This was opportunit. I tightened the sling on my sniper's rifle and stepped back into the shadows on the platform and let loose a few rounds. I hadn't noticed up to this time that a Fox Company buddy had followed me up the stairway. He leaned out the window and banged away with his M-1 exposing himself to all those troops. I exclaimed that we should get the hell out of there and we backtracked down the stairway in record time. We ran out of the building just in time to hear a big explosion, and looked up at what was our shooting perch. They had just blown out that whole wall. That buddy, and I can't recall his name, really saved my life that day by firing out that window. If I had remained up there alone, I probably would have been confident that I was hidden and would have lingered long enough to be discovered. He did me a favor, and didn't realize it, by banging away showing the enemy where the shots were coming from. After leaving the building we kept veering to the left in the direction of more shooting sounds and there we were able to make contact with the rest of the squad."[103]

Stoddard's sighting of a horse drawn wagon was not unusual. Many people think about tank (panzer) battalions when they think about the German Army. But the German Army had less trucks then the American Army. The German Army used many horses to pull supply wagons and artillery guns. A German Infantry battalion had 11 motor vehicles, 45 horse drawn wagons and 120 horses. An American Infantry Battalion had 40 motor vehicles.[104]

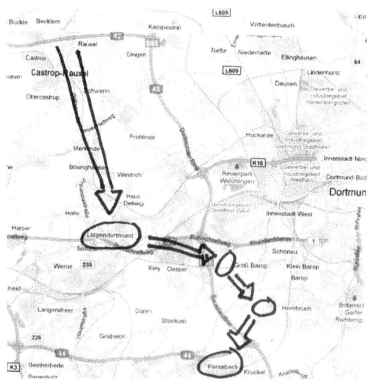

Google Map of Persebeck, Germany[105]

Fox Company's final objective is Persbeck which is at the southern part of this map.

Nathan Henn wrote of his memories of the last battles. "From Rutgers Castle we worked our way slowly and surely toward the outskirts of Dortmund. When the 95th ID went through Dortmund they marched through without opposition. The city was an empty shell, battered from air attack. When the defenses around the city crumbled it was all over. Other units of our Division proceeded south to the Ruhr River. We merely "mopped up". This term sounds insignificant but it means lives of men and much suffering."[106]

Red Carr remembers the action at another castle with a moat. This must have been a different castle from Rutgers/ Bladenhorst, since 2nd platoon was in reserve when Fox attacked Rutgers/ Bladenhorst and the Germans were dug in outside Rutgers/Bladenhorst. Also the moat at Rutgers/Bladenhorst was only partly filled. Also Earl Adams, Red Carr's squad leader, told his son about swimming a moat to get to a castle. As Red approached the bridge across the moat, the Germans blew it up. The blast knocked him down and he lost hearing in one ear. Concrete rained down on him. The squad had to swim across the moat. As the squad crossed the moat, one squad member announced he did not know how to swim. Adams pulled the man from the moat but lost his M1 rifle in the water. Dick Phillips and Carr crossed the moat and attacked the castle. A German threw a hand grenade out a window. Dick picked it up and threw it back in the window where it blew up. Carr captured a Major and about a dozen paratroopers. Carr relieved the Major of his weapon and bayonet. He was able to keep the weapon and has passed the weapon on to his son in Minnesota.[107]

On April 9th another unit from the 291st was allowed to take the town of Castrop-Rauxel, while Fox advanced toward Lutgen-Dortmund. Here the 291st Infantry relieved the 289th Infantry Regiment. Fox spent the night in Lutgen-Dortmund, which a pile of rubble caused by constant bombing by the Americans during the day and the British at night.

Fox continued the attack south on April 10th. Fox attacked the town of Eichlinghofen meeting little resistance. We were consolidating our forces when a civilian came to Cox and reported that there was a bunch of armed soldiers up at the City Hall. Cox was getting a group of men together to check out the report when LT Jones volunteered to lead the group. Jones always wanted to be in the middle of the action. Soon Jones was back loaded down with lugers, P38's and an assortment of weapons. He reported the soldiers turned out to be the whole police force, waiting to give themselves up. Everyone got their choice of a souvenir weapon. Later that evening Fox had a little fire fight over the small town of Menglinghausen and spent the night there.

On April 11th, fox was moving southward, meeting little delaying action now and then. We had learned how to deal with these things. S/Sgt Porter of the 60mm mortar section, Weapons platoon had the reputation of being able to drop a 60mm mortar shell into a gallon bucket at 200 yards. The Germans were retreating so fast they did not have time to dig in so a mortar shell close to their position would cause them to high tail it out of there. Mission accomplished!

We were in a mining area, where we would pass a high hill of stuff that a mining company piles up when they dig deep into the ground. We stopped for the night. We had the word that we would be soon be pinched out by other units. That night LTC Drain ordered LT Stegen's 1st platoon to be attached to K Company of 3rd Battalion 291st Infantry Regiment for the next days attack.

LT Bob Stegen tried for several hours to find Company K but never linked up with them. For about 4 hours Stegen did not see enemy in front of him, so he lead his platoon across an open area of about 30 yards with the goal of getting to a rail road embankment. The Germans fired rounds from a 20 mm canon used to shoot at aircraft. Stegen was wounded and PFC Kay Edge, who was behind Stegen, was killed. Sgt Shea was also killed. Stegen was hit in the upper leg. Stegen laid on the battlefield for some time before a medic used a fireman's carry to get Stegen to an aid station.[108] He would rejoin Fox two months later at Camp Baltimore, France.

On April 12th Fox was moving into town of Persebeck when Cox got a report that one of our men had seen Germans in strength digging in near a large house. Cox went into a two story civilian operated hospital and climbed the stairs to the second floor. Cox had a good view of the whole area. There were railroad tracks running east west about 400 yards in front of the hospital. About 600 yards further to the southwest was the house. We could see the Germans digging in. Their helmets were shining in the sun. S/Sgt Porter was setting up his mortars on the north side of the railroad embankment. Cox told him when he was ready to commence firing. The light machine guns were also setting up on the railroad embankment. Cox could see everything through his field glasses. The first two rounds fell short. The Germans stopped digging and ran into the house. Cox reported the situation to LTC Drain and he said it was Fox's target so we should take it.

LT Denton advised Cox that we were using a civilian hospital for directing military operations and that we should move on. There were a lot of old patients in the hospital, all watching us. A couple of doctors were there too but they did not complain.

Cox could not see much of the town from the hospital window. But after we moved on we could see it was a fairly good size town. LT Jones and his 2nd platoon moved through the town to sweep out whatever opposition he encountered. Cox moved under an overpass to a house overlooking the German strong point. Cox observed an 8 man German patrol moving up a road away from their house, toward the other end of town.

Cox called Jones on the radio and advised him of the patrol. Jones called back that he sighted the patrol and would set up an ambush. Cox watched through his field glasses as the German patrol got closer.

Then Cox saw the Germans scatter and hit the ditches. Cox knew someone had fired too soon or they had spotted the Americans. Some of the men later said LT Jones jumped out into the middle of the road and started firing. Jones knows now that he should have let them get a lot closer. The 8 man German patrol made it back to their cover.

In the mean time Fox was getting ready to attack the strongpoint. The Germans had an artillery piece somewhere to the rear of their house. Every few minutes they would fire a round but they never got close to us. Most would land way behind us.

The road, that ran by Cox's position and on by some other houses, was a sunken road where we could move around unobserved by the Germans. The house next to our house was about 75 yards away. Every once in awhile, the German's would fire a 20mm automatic weapon and the rounds ricochet off the wall of the nearby house. None of us got hurt by that weapon but we got a kick out of watching the 20mm shells hitting the wall.

Sgt Moss was acting 3rd Platoon Leader with LT Thompson wounded and LT Chitwood still recuperating in an Army hospital. 3rd platoon moved into an assault position, Moss asked Cox to go with them and Cox said yes. Cox had been calling for smoke to screen their movements several times. But the artillery always said they had a prior mission.

Our tanks were not available yet so Cox asked the FO to call for fire on the house using point detonating fuse instead of Pozit fuse (which burst in the air) The artillery still said they had a prior mission.

Cox climbed up in the attic to get a better look at the terrain around the house. There was a large hole in the front part of the roof. Cox had to get in the prone position to get close enough to see what he wanted to see. Just when he was settled down he heard a shell coming incoming. Cox knew it was going to be close. In fact he thought it would hit the roof and he would be a goner.

There was a tree right beside the house. The shell hit the tree. Sgt Moss and a number of his men were under that tree. The tree burst mortally wounded Russell Cross and killed William Ford instantly. It wounded 4 or 5 men. Ed Letourneau was one of the wounded. Cox was told about Cross and that he was lying under the overpass hit bad. Cox was down out of the attic very fast and went to Cross. He turned him over and saw a big hole in his back. A piece of shrapnel had hit him. It seemed he was breathing through that hole. Cox knew he was dying so he tried to comfort him telling him he was gonna be ok. Cross died as Cox was holding him.

Sgt Moss was shaking and almost crying. Cox knew he was shell shocked. Moss said he could not lead his men in an attack anymore. Cox sent him to the Battalion aid station. He rejoined Fox at Erndtebruck three weeks later.

Cox called LTC Drain and advised him of the situation. Stegen was attached to another unit. Jones was engaged in a different part of town and Fox did not have enough men to sustain the attack. Drain understood and turned the job over to Easy Company. The tanks had arrived and started blasting at the German's house with direct fire from two 76mm cannons. Then low and below, after about 20 minutes of cannon fire, here came the artillery smoke to screen Easy Company's advance.

Out came the white flags and the Germans surrendered. Easy Company marched about 30 prisoners out in front of us. Cox was so mad he almost fired on them. He would have but was concerned he would hit one of the soldiers marching them out. It all seemed so useless because the war was almost over.

Fox company continued to attack south capturing Eichlinghofen in a fire fight and capturing Menglinghausen in a night attack, both on April 11th. Fox then attacked southwest to Persebeck on April 12th. This was Fox Company's last day of combat. On this map Persebeck in marked with a red balloon in the bottom center of the map. Menglinghausen is northeast of Persebeck. Eichlinghofen is northwest of Menglinghausen. Eichlinghofen and Menglinghausen are today small towns that do not show on many maps.

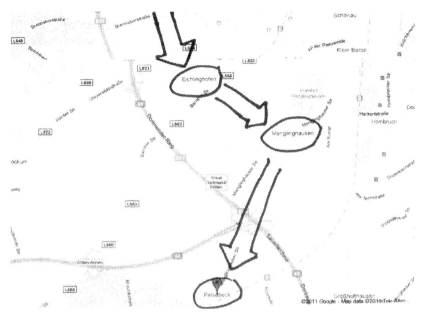

Google Map of Persebeck, Germany showing last 3 objectives[109]

It is normal for an Infantry battalion to attack in a zigzag manner, as the objective was to seize key pieces of terrain from the enemy.

The next day we learned President Roosevelt had died on April 12th. While Fox was on the attack on April 12th, the 95th Infantry division entered Dortmund and found the enemy defenses had fallen. 2nd Battalion continued to attack to the Ruhr River. The Regiment defended the north bank of the Ruhr River until on at 1700 hours, April 14th the Regiment was relieved by elements of the 79th ID. A total of 1018 Germans were captured by the 291st Infantry Regiment in the Ruhr since April 1st.[110]

By now the German Army was pushed south of the Ruhr River and was surrounded again. Most of the Allied Army had by passed it and had attacked to the east to the Elbe River. The German Army Group Commander, General Model told his forces to try to break out to the east. But most of his Army was surrendering. Unwilling to surrender, Model shot himself.[111]

OCCUPATION DUTY

Cpl Ray Stoddard's main military duty was to patrol a cross road and check passports. He was to look for papers indicating the person was Gestapo. No one ever was but there were many displaced persons moving East.

AFTER REACHING THE RUHR River, the 75th ID was given on April 15, 1945 the mission to govern part of Germany. Fox and the 75th ID moved several times. One time Fox's area included a prisoner of war camp for Italians. Fox was happy to move into a town called Erndtebruck where they governed the area for about 30 days. Erndtebruck was in the German area of North Rhine-Westphalia. Erndtebruck is northeast of Siegen and east of Koln (Cologne). Fox was issued an America flag to be raised over the town to signal the Americans were in charge. Ted Cox held on to this flag and it brought to many Fox reunions after the war.

Near Erndtebruck was a displaced persons (DP) camp, with about 125 men and 25 women. The women had separate housing and men were not suppose to enter the women's area. The DP's were Russians and were used by the Germans as slave labors. They lived in poorly constructed barracks. Living conditions were terrible. A stream ran through the middle of the camp. The stream was their only source of water for drinking, cooking and bathing. They had outhouses for their toilet. There was barbed wire around the camp to try to keep the Russians in their camp. But every day they would cut the wire and slip out. Cox hired an Italian woman, whose German Lieutenant Colonel husband was missing on the Russian front, to be his interpreter. Several times a day Germans would come to Cox to complain about the DP's. The DP's were accosting the German s on the street and stealing bicycles from them. Cox's sympathies were with the DP's. But one time some DP's obtained some Mauser 8 mm rifles. They strip the rifles down to the trigger mechanism and the barrel. They sawed off the barrel, leaving 3 to 4 inches. We called them zip guns. They really terrorized the German civilians with those weapons. Cox knew he had to disarm these guys. They were crazy and not afraid of anything. Cox took 3 men with M1 Garand's and took each of the 3 armed men, one at a time, to a safe place and disarmed them. It got a little nasty one time when the Russian would not give up his zip gun. We had to convince him that we were going to shoot him on the spot if he did not give up his weapon. He finally gave up his weapon and we did not have to shoot him. But it almost came to that. Before Fox Company left Erndtebruk for France, the Russian government sent a train and they loaded up for the ride back to Russia. We offered to take some of them back to the States but not a one indicated they wanted to defect.

Ray remembers moving Germans from their houses and Fox men moving in. Ray was in a two story house with a forest behind it. He and others had fun going back deep into the forest. They found a stream and used hand grenades to harvest fish for their meals. In Ray's house there was a false wall hiding a roomful of potatoes and onions, which Ray cooked most days to add to his diet. Ray's main military duty was to patrol a crossroad and check passports. He was to look for papers indicating the person was Gestapo. No one ever was but there were many DP's moving East. After what they been through they were in sorry shape. The DP's had to scrounge to stay alive. Soldiers shared what they had with those that asked.[112]

Reither remembered Victory in Europe day, May 8th as not too exciting. Fox did have a great meal in the mess hall and had beer. Reither said the men were still sweating out being sent to the War in the Pacific. Dick Siakel remembers on May 8th because he was still eighteen. He turned nineteen on May 10th.[113]

The May 18, 1945 issue of the *Mule* had an article about Fox Company's Rec Hall and Bar. When the reporter arrived, PFC Dick Dietze was playing piano. PFC Lyle Watts and PFC Guy Stone were serving beer. The veranda off the bar was the most popular spot in the Inn.[114] Ted Cox stated Fox had taken over a German Gasthaus, a local village restaurant and bar, to be its mess hall.

During this time Dan Mooney and Jack Reese supplied the Mess Hall with fresh venison. They also brought in trout. Dick Siakel said Mooney and Reese would shoot their M1's at trout, stunning the trout. Siakel had a picture of Mooney and Reese with a string of trout.[115]

Reese took Cox on one deer hunting trip. Cox had hunted deer in Northeast Louisiana, starting at the age of 15. At 4am Reese, Mooney, and Cox drove about two and a half miles up a hill over looking the valley. The hunters occupied a deer stand that was built like a large platform on stilts about 10 feet tall. There were steps to climb to get to the platform, which was 8 feet wide. There was a sign on the end of the platform next to the steps which had "Herman Goering" printed on it. The platform had comfortable bench seats where we could watch for deer in the clearing in front of the stand. Cox had his carbine and Reese and Mooney had their M1's. Reese gave Cox his M1 because he did not think the carbine had enough knock down power to bring down a deer. It was about daylight when Cox spotted a deer move into the clearing, about 1000 yards down the valley. Cox knew it was too far away but took a shot and missed. About 15 minutes later a 6 point Buck walked into the clearing about 50 yards away. Cox fired and the deer started running. Cox fired 4 more shots and the deer went down. Reese and Mooney left their M1's in the deer stand but Cox took his carbine. Cox had hunted deer enough to know they sometimes get up and run. Then you have to track the deer down and have to drag the deer a longer distance. Sure enough when they got within 20 feet of the buck, it jumped up and began running away. Cox fired one shot and the buck was down for good. The hunters found all five shot's from the M1 had hit the deer. But with steel jacketed bullets all 5 bullets went through the deer's body. The carbine shot hit the buck in the back of the neck, breaking it, killing the deer instantly.

About May 20, 1945 higher headquarters said Fox could pick two enlisted men that could take a 30 day leave back to the United States. Pappy French and Joe Affeldt were picked. They never returned to Fox because the powers that be thought the war would be over soon.

Photo by John Fetrow. The war left much of Europe in ruins.

Company meeting after April 12th where Captain Cox tells the men about occupation duty. General Eisenhower had ordered no fraternizing with the Germans. You could not even shake hands with them.

S/SGT Percy Brown being awarded the Bronze Star. LT Denton presents the award and on right LT Chitwood reads the award.

In the month of April PFC Jennings Brown and PFC Robert Thomas were awarded the bronze star.

The following pictures taken at Erndtebruck, Germany and later at Camp Baltimore, France show the men of Fox Company relaxing and enjoying life after being at War. As General Omar Bradley wrote in his tribute to the infantryman, a rifleman lived with the constant threat of death or serious injury. Only victory would end the threat to their well being.[116] These pictures show men happy to be alive and waiting to go home.

Captain Cox, LT Denton and LT Jones after the war

PFC Phillips, LT Denton, S/Sgt McKay, Cpl Eddington
HQ's men after the war at Erndtebruck

Cpl Brown and Cpl Mumford were two of the Company Medics assigned
from Battalion Headquarters. This is probably a picture of Brown

Cpl Mumford with Russian music box and Longo from Second
platoon. Mumford was usually assigned to 2nd platoon.

THE COOKS

*Front row: PFC John Fetrow, Sgt George Grubb, PFC Tweedle
Back row: Laterman, S/Sgt Don Nadeau, Cpl T/5 Andy
Anderson and Cpl T/5 Charles Holt. PFC Tweedle was
the company barber with other assigned duties.*

*S/SGT Don Nadeau and Cpl Eddington with
car PFC Hank Arend had fixed*

PFC Hank Arend in his jeep after the war

Around May 29th Fox boarded boxcars and rode the train through Germany, Holland Belgium to arrive in France on June 1st. The train's boxcars were called 40 and 8 because they could hold 40 men or 8 horses. We called them GI Pullman's.

Left to right Sgt Huff, PFC Royston, unknown

2nd Platoon buddies Hayes, Clausius, and Wolpert

Edgar "Ted" Cox and Scott Adams

*Earl Adams and Del Goodyear next to a German Train 1945.
Adams came home in the first week of May 1946 and married his
high school sweetheart on June 13th Goodyear was his best man.*

*Left to Right Andy Schaft, Hank Arend and unknown,
After the war Hank married Andy's sister-in-law.*

PFC James Floyd Davis in Germany. A German half timbered house is in the background.

CAMP BALTIMORE, FRANCE
AND GOING HOME
★ ★ ★

Ed went to Chicago to visit John Klimek's mother. John's mother was so upset that her son died and Ed survived, she shut the door in Ed's face

AFTER BEING RELIEVED BY fresh units, Fox Company and 291st Infantry Regiment moved to Camp Baltimore about 25 miles southeast of Rheims, France. Many men were able to take leave to England and Switzerland. Soldiers were issued rations cards signed by Captain Edgar Cox to allow them to buy personal items at the Army Exchange.

Fox Company area Camp Baltimore.

The Company had large tents for the men. The tents were winterized to be warm. For awhile they had dirt floors. One of the company men was good at midnight requisitioning and soon the company had plywood floors. Sidewalks were made out of metal strips used to make Air Corps runways.

Camp Baltimore was near Rheims France.
This is the Rheims Cathedral

While at Camp Baltimore, Fox Company men were given leave to travel through Europe. Rheims and Paris were visited by many. Some went to Switzerland. Others went to England. Ray Stoddard was able to go to Scotland and play golf on the famous Saint Andrews course. Ray found an interesting way to pay for the trip. His friend Nathan Henn did not smoke and gave Ray a carton of cigarettes. Ray sold the cigarettes in Paris and made enough money to finance his trip to Scotland. LT Bob Stegen recovered from his wounds and returned to Fox Company at Camp Baltimore. Ted Cox and Stegen shared a tent and became fast friends. Bob taught Ted how to play cribbage. All the other guys would go to Rheims but Ted and Bob were content to stay in camp and play cribbage.

Many men wanted to go on weekend passes to Paris with Ed Letourneau, because he could speak French. Ed found he had friends he never knew before.[117]

Ed Neville remembers traveling to through France and Switzerland with Earnest Benner.[118]

Sgt Adamski and PFC Laskoski, HQ personnel clerks in Paris

Cpl Ray Stoddard at the wheel of his worn torn jeep in Suippes, France. PFC Tom Taylor is the passenger.

S/Sgt Earl Adams, Capt. Harvey Cannon, S/Sgt Del Goodyear, After the War at Camp Baltimore, France. Cannon was the first platoon leader for Second Platoon and took over Company E during the War.

Camp Baltimore, France June 6, 1945
Standing left: Longo, standing right Else (carried BAR)
Kneeling left: Adams, kneeling right: Hardy

Sgt Doug Huff assistant squad leader and S/Sgt Adams

PFC Dick Phillips (squad scout), S/Sgt Earl Adams squad leader
3rd squad 2nd platoon, Camp Baltimore 1945. Adams told his family
his squad had less casualties than other squads. But the records
show the squad had 1 killed and 6 wounded. But other squads by
the end of the Colmar Pocket had loss 9 men and both leaders.

Dick Siakel stated Camp Baltimore was the site of World War 1 battlefield. Siakel said you could see the outline of trenches with their dog leg paths. Siakel said Earl Adams worked for the camp's Provost Marshal and had a jeep. One day Adams took Siakel and other soldiers to see the remains of a World War 1 airplane in the forest. Siakel said the plane looked like a Sopwith Camel. Siakel also saw the remains of an artillery piece with wooden spokes for its tires.[119]

1ˢᵗ Squad, 2nd Platoon men after the war. All are PFC's except were noted. Top Row: Sam Smith, S/Sgt Nathan Henn, Buck Schaefer, Dan Mooney. Center Row: Dick Siakel, T/5 Red Watland, Fred Shank, Jack Reese. Front Row: Harvey Glenn, Lowell Murphy, Ron Collette.

Nate Henn and German POW, Karl Arnold, who helped at the library

2nd Platoon men at Camp Baltimore, knelling Doug Huff on the left and Charles Lewellen on the right. Del Goodyear standing on the right. Bill "Ski" Szwaczkowski second from the right.

3rd Platoon men

Weapons Platoon. Benner, Leonard, Forehand, Minarsich, Thomas

Weapons Platoon at Camp Baltimore. Back Row: Minarsick, Benner, Neville, Leonard, Thomas. Front Row: Lachat, Wethington, Johnson, Tarasevich, Tuhacek

Ed Neville Mortar Squad Leader

Fox men playing cards in a Quonset hut at Camp Baltimore

In the April 27th, 1945 issue of the 75th Infantry Division newspaper The *Mule*, Major General John Anderson, Commander of the XVI Corps, had praise for the 75th ID. He stated the effective screening of the Rhine River allowed troops and supplies to be assembled out of the view of the Germans. Also the aggressive patrolling and constant observation developed great intelligence on the Germans. He also stated that the attack made by the 75th ID after the lead Divisions lost their impetus, was made against strong opposition by the enemy. The 75th ID helped clear the enemy from the Ruhr Industrial area and drove the enemy south of the Ruhr River. All of this was completed in a much shorter period of time than had been estimated.[120]

Richard DeBruyn wrote about how flashbacks could be triggered. "Down through the years one occurrence or another gave me 'flashbacks' to those bitter days of the 'Battle of the Bulge'. December 1944. This year is no different!"

"Last week, while browsing through a religious publication I was startled by a particular photograph taken near one of their local missions. Startled is hardly the word! If the overhead wires were removed, there is an exact replica of a snow covered, forested crossroads encountered in an attack through the Ardennes. Memories came in a flood."

"The snow is unmarked except for a single set of tracks on the road. A cluster of shrubbery near the intersection, heavily snow laden, resembles the partially camouflaged tank firing down the lumber road to the right. Deep shadows form the shapes of crewmen atop the turret. On the embankment, nearby, other shadows form the outline of dug-in infantry and gun crews."

"Beyond the intersection, vehicles are parked on the road shoulder, so heavily covered with snow. The shapes are hardly discernable. These resemble the knocked-out tracks and armor we passed. Across the road from these is that burned-out farm building."

"Today's weather makes it all seem so real and I go through it all over again. Memories are on me and I get that gut-knotting feeling; a combination of cold, fear and anxiety. I am extremely exhausted and so tired from the constant moves and lack of sleep. I feel that numbing, bone-chilling cold. Shimmering ice crystals form in the sub-zero air. The air freezes and tightens in my nostrils. My ears ache. Each intake of breath sears my lungs. As I breathe, ice forms and coats my face and clothing. Perspiration trails an icy path down my body. I have never been so cold. The hands and feet are numb."

"Snow crackles sharply underfoot as we plod along. Our bodies are bent beneath the heavy load. Dense fog forms just above the ground. Soon only the lower half of the man's legs ahead are visible. Forms become disembodied wraiths in its depths. It is eerie! In the distance, artillery pieces thump their message."

"Shells "crump" upon impact, sounds muted by the elements. Occasional fragments moan as they flutter by. Mortar rounds sound like sacks of chains being dropped as they crash in the near hollows. Fragments 'whirr' about, spending themselves in the trees. A deadly 'BRRP-BRRP!' of an automatic weapons gives a shudder to the spine. Someone shrieks horribly as he is hit. Every foreign sound adds to the fear. The very air has an aura of a slaughter house. I force myself to stay steady and firm through it all. I partially succeed."

"All these years and the old nightmare is back! Now that I have written it down, I feel much better."[121]

Finally after being hit by two atomic bombs, the Japanese surrendered and Fox men could stop worrying about being sent to the Pacific. In an August 16, 1945 issue of the *Stars and Stripes*. Winston Churchill stated the Atomic bomb had ended the war. He also said the war plans for invading Japan had estimated a million Americans and a quarter of a million British soldiers would have died in the battle to control Japan.[122]

The September 21, 1945 issue of the Division newspaper, The *Mule* stated a 75th ID Association was started to provide a post-war link with war time comrades. Membership fees were two dollars. Brigadier General Mickle, now the division commander was issued the first membership card.[123]

The front page of the first newsletter from the 75th Infantry Division veterans association. Map shows path of movement of the 75th during the war.[124]

The *Mule* on September 21, 1945 also stated the G3 section had put together a day by day history of the division in the European Theater of Operation (EPO). 3 maps showing the Battle in the Ardennes, the Colmar Pocket and the Battle for the Ruhr would be included. Copies of these maps are included with this history. Each man was to get one copy.[125]

This September issue also had a picture of the starting eleven for the division football team. Del Goodyear was a starting guard. The list of team members also included Lloyd Fowler and Joe Hessel. Ted Cox remembers the football team was housed for several months in an excellent hotel in the city of Rheims. Many men wished they played football.[126]

The *Mule* also had an article stating the 75th ID was schedule to sail to the states on October 15th 1945. But most men of the 75th ID would not be going home with the Division. The Army had developed a point system. Enlisted men had to have 60 points and officers a 100 points to sail with the Division. High point men from other Divisions would fill out the ships. Major Dick Winters who had become famous from the book and TV movie the Band of Brothers was transferred from the 101st Airborne Division to command the 2nd Battalion, 290th Infantry Regiment and sailed on the trip home on November 1, 1945.[127]

The point system gave extra points to married men with children. Ted Cox and James Davis for example had children and sailed back to the States in December 1945. Men who did not have enough points were transferred to the Assembly Area Command (AAC). The AAC ran 17 camps in France each named for a US city. After the 75th Division sailed with high point men, the men of Fox Company were split up for other duty by the AAC. For example John Fetrow was reassigned to a Quartermaster unit. Dick Phillips and Raymond Bagley were assigned to Grave Registration units. Dick Scatena had two German POW's to help him process photography film. He said the soldiers wanted to have their film developed before going home because they did not want their families to see some of the pictures of the war. Dick also had a task which he found hard to do. It was his responsibility to send personal items of men who were killed back home to families. Bob Stegen was given the job to escort was brides between Brussels and Paris. Ray Stoddard had a job at Camp Baltimore motor pool.

At Camp Baltimore, Ed Letourneau worked in the Base Exchange, a small store, where soldiers could come and buy things like cigarettes, soap, tooth brushes. Ed finally left France in January 1946. After getting home,

Ed went to Chicago to visit John Klimek's mother. John's mother was so upset that her son had died and Ed survived, she shut the door in Ed's face and would not talk to him. Ed was bothered by this event.[128]

Fox men kept their rifles for awhile. One of the duties Fox men had while still a division at Baltimore was guard duty and the men were armed for that twenty-four hour misery. Ray Stoddard recalled going on half-day trips in an open truck to pick up German prisoners and deliver them to our area camp for assignment to KP and other janitorial duties. The back end of the truck was packed with maybe forty prisoners and Ray with them armed with a carbine. Luckily they were complacent and looking forward to camp duties

Picture of Fox Company men marching off for guard duty.

Ray Stoddard remembers that it was a sad day when the 75th broke up. We were ordered to remove our 75th patches from the left shoulder and put on the "OISE patch. The 75th patch went on the right shoulder. Once we were a part of the new OISE command, discipline fell apart. Most Fox company men came home by May 1946.[129]

Logo of the 75th Infantry Newspaper The Mule in France[130]

Picture taken by Ray Stoddard.
Barracks bags lined by soldiers prior to getting on a troop ship to sail home.

A picture of the troop ship in which Ray Stoddard came
back to the United States in February 1946.

Ray like most soldiers shipped out of LeHarve, France. Ray took these pictures with his Brownie Bullet camera. When Ray got sick on a visit to London in November 1944, Captain Drake dropped Ray from the company roster and had all of Ray's belongings packed up in a barracks bag. The barracks bag was shipped out into limbo. While at Camp Baltimore, Ray put in a trace request and his bag was located near

Paris. Ray took a jeep from the motor pool and retrieved his bag. All of his belongings were there to include his camera.[131]

The Atlantic Ocean can be rough. Ray Stoddard and John Fetrow came home in February 1946 when the seas were rough and stormy. In the mess hall you had to hold on to your plate. When troop ships arrived in New York harbor they were met with blaring horns and whistles from other ship in the harbor. The Statue of Liberty was a beautiful sight. After leaving the troop ships soldiers were sent to near by Army camps. They were given new uniforms and fed a steak dinner with all the trimmings. Ted Cox remembers that after leaving the troop ship he saw a hot dog stand. He ate five or six hot dogs with lots of mustard, something he had not had in 17 months. Most soldiers were sent home by train and bus. Soldiers on the West Coast flew home in aircraft such as the C47. The men of Fox were able to call home so they can be met by family at their point of arrival at a train or bus station. At home some went back to the job they had before the war. Some went to work on the family farm. Many used the GI Bill and went to college. Transition to college was not easy. While there were many veterans only a few had been in the Infantry and had experienced war up close.

Being busy fighting the war, Infantry companies did not have time to submit many men for awards. After the war, General Marshall learned the Infantry had 9.3 per cent of the awards even though the Infantry had 75.02 per cent of the Army casualties in Europe, while the Air Corps had a 9.36 per cent of the casualties and 83.32 per cent of the awards.[132] So General Marshall gave the order that every man who earned a Combat Infantry Men's Badge or a Combat Medics Badge would be awarded a Bronze Star for valor.[133] The news of the award spread slowly through the veterans, who had to write and request the award. Maurice "Red" Carr is probably the last to get the award. He learned about the award during a Veteran Affairs review of his records and finally got the award in 2004.[134]

In January 2011, Ray Stoddard received a medal from the French Government, naming him a Knight of the Legion of Honor for his actions during World War II. Ray had read about the award in the 75th Division Veterans Association newsletter. Only 100 awards are made by France each year and they are not given posthumously. It took Ray 4 years to get the award. Ray said the award represents all the guys in Fox Company.[135]

Norma and Red Carr a few years after being awarded his Bronze Star.

The 75th ID lives on from the early 1950's to the present, 2012. It is believed that the 75th ID was picked to be an Army Reserve Division because of its World War II history of training soldiers. In the 1950's, the 75th Division Maneuver Area Command (MAC) was organized to control and conduct large scale military exercises. The 291st Infantry Regiment was then located in Oklahoma.

The Army stopped doing large scale maneuvers in the 1970's. In the 1980's war training started using computers. In the build up for the Gulf war in 1990, the 75th MAC trained battalions and brigades deploying to Saudi Arabia using computer simulations to generate battle information for staffs to react to.

In 1990's the 75th MAC became the 75th Training Support (TS) with five brigades. The Regimental designations were assigned to the Brigades. The 3rd Brigade that had the 291st as its heritage was to support training of Aviation battalions. The 289th Regiment was aligned with 1st Brigade that supported Infantry training. In 2003 to 2007 1st Brigade sent trainers from the 1st Brigade, 75th to Iraq to help build their new Army. In October 2009, 160 trainers in 6 detachments spent a year in Iraq helping to train their Army.

In 2009 the Division was renamed 75th Battle Command Training Division (BCTD) provides Battle Command Staff Training (BCST) for commanders and their staffs at battalion and brigade echelons of command. Organized into five Battle Command Training Brigades (BCTB) with subordinate Battle Command Training Groups (BCTG), units are located in California, Colorado, Texas, Oklahoma, Illinois, Alabama, Rhode Island and New Jersey, BCTBs and their BCTGs are strategically positioned to provide regional support to Reserve and Active Component units deploying to the Iraq and Afghan combat zones. But the Regimental designations, such as the 291st, are no longer used. On October 1, 2011, the Division was renamed 75th Training Division Mission Command.

Ray Stoddard was selected in the summer of 2011 to go on a Honor Flight trip to Washington DC to view the World War 2 memorial. When Ray returned members of the 3rd Brigade, 75th Training Division (Mission Command) were at the airport to welcome the veterans of World War 2. From this meeting Ray was invited to the Brigade Dining Out on November 5, 2011. Ray was given the honor of sitting at the head table. Two other veterans, Earl Beese and James Butz, from the 75th ID in World War 2 attended the dinner.

Cpl James Butz H-290th, Cpl Ray Stoddard
F-291st, and PFC Earl Beese, C-291st

Ruth Henn Krosin and Ray Stoddard, August 31, 2011, at the World War 2 Memorial. Ruth is the daughter of Nate Henn.

In 2010, Ruth and her son Richard met Ted Cox when Ted went on a Honor Flight to see the World War 2 Memorial. Honor Flight is a non-profit that takes veterans to see their memorial in Washington DC. Priority is given to World War 2 veterans[136]

Ted Cox with his son, Phillip, his daughter, Elizabeth, her daughter, Julia at the World War 2 Memorial in 2010.

Ted Cox, behind Ted is his son, Phillip, and to the right Richard Krosin, Grandson of Nate Henn. The history of Fox Company is being passed down through the generations.

CONCLUSION

✶ ✶ ✶

Fox held a reunion every year from 1988. In 2006 they had their last reunion in St. Charles, MO attended by nine Fox men and one associate. Fox men still keep in touch, they don't do anymore traveling. They had their last hurrah!

TED COX REMEMBERS ON April 12, 1945 Fox Company fought its last battle on German soil. They did not know it at the time but they were being pinched out by other units. We sensed that the Germans were getting beat on all fronts. According to the Stars and Stripes, they were surrendering in droves, wanting to be captured by the Americans rather than the Russians.

Fox men would always go out of their way to help one another. As the commanding officer, I could always depend on them to do their duty, whatever danger it might entail. Camaraderie that exists between the the men of Fox was evident through the three campaigns in which we fought.

From our brief stay at Erndtebruck, to the months spent at Camp Baltimore, Fox men showed their friendship for each other, whether pulling guard duty, on a trip to Switzerland or just hanging out.

After World War 2 was finished and we all went our separate ways, to school or back to the old job. We often wondered what the other guys were doing. In 1980, Cox got a call from Bob Stegen. Cox had moved from Springhill, LA to Magnolia, AR and finally to Saint Charles, MO. Bob had been trying to locate him. He had phoned the Mayor of Springhill, who did not know where Cox lived. But he knew Cox's wife's sister. Bob talked to her and got Cox's phone number. Ted and Bob got together later that year.

In 1987 Cox read in the American Legion magazine about a 75th Division reunion in Las Vegas. Cox contacted Stegen and Foster Jones and met in Las Vegas for the reunion. The only other Fox man there was Hank Arend. Cox got a roster from Jim Warmouth, the 75th Division secretary. Cox found about twenty Fox men listed with their addresses. Cox wrote them and set up a Fox reunion. In 1989 Fox held a reunion in Louisville. KY at Cox's daughter's house. Twenty five Fox men and their wives in attendance. One man who came with his wife was Merle Johnson. Merle looked like death warmed over. His wife told Cox that Merle had cancer of the lungs and only had a few days to live. But he had to live long enough to come to the Fox reunion. She wrote two weeks later that Merle had passed away. He was so happy that he got to see some of his buddies. This is an example of the camaraderie between Fox men.

Fox held reunions every year. In 2006 the last one was held in Saint Charles, MO. Cox told the men that he could not travel anymore. Parkinson was taking its toll. It was quite an emotional farewell party. Nine Fox men were there all that was left of the original 35 who came to reunions. The Fox men were Stegen, Reither, Craig, Siakel, Putnam, Fetrow, Chitwood, Stoddard and Cox. Wives that attended were Thelma Fetrow, Ina Putnam, Sandi Siakel Nancy Stoddard and Mary Cox. There were three Fox widows at the reunion: Mrs. Foster Jones, Mrs. Beryl Lantz and Mrs. Buck Schaeffer.

Bill Davis, son of James Davis, an associate member also came.

The Fox men left still keep in touch. But no more traveling. They had their last hurrah!

APPENDIX A

CASUALTY LIST

MEMBERS OF FOX COMPANY, 2nd battalion, 291st Infantry Regiment killed or wounded in action against the Germans in World War II. Some dates may be off by a day. This happens when the injury does not get reported until the next day's morning report.

Date	Rank	Killed in Action	Wounded in Action
Jan. 15,'45	Cpl		Walter Clausius
	PFC		Frank Alcott
Jan 16	2LT	Paul K. Bowman	
	PFC		John A. Mack
	PFC		Harry S. Singer
	PFC		Walter K. Thabit
Jan 17	PFC	John Hughes	
	PFC		Grover Hardy
	PFC		Daniel Mooney
Jan 19	2LT		William F. Hanser
	S/Sgt		Robert Berkebile
	Pvt	Robert D. Benish	

Date	Rank	Killed in Action	Wounded in Action
	Pvt		Kay D. Edge
	Pvt		Alexander F. Shannon
	Pvt		John J. Gettuse
	PFC		Allen W. Craig
	S/Sgt		Merle V. Johnson
	PFC		Rex A. Williams
Jan 20	PFC	John H Klimek	
	PFC		William C. Evrard
	Pvt		Rex A. Williams
Jan 24	T/Sgt		John F. Karlowski
	PFC		Nathan Henn
Jan 25	S/Sgt	Donnie W. Glasscock	
	PFC	Hugh McDermott	
	PFC	Ridley W. Meeks	
	PFC	Bert W. Nelson	
	PFC	James S. Winebrenner	
	Capt		James S Drake
	PFC		Jack R. Hudson
	PFC		John L. Longo
	PFC		Richard J. Thibault
Jan 25	S/Sgt		Rupert K. Buchanen
	S/Sgt		Russell L. Kime
	PFC		Richard DeBruyn
	PFC		Thomas E. Royster
	PFC		Lyle H. Watts
Jan 31	Pvt	Alfred S. Freeman	
	PFC		Calvin W. Hood
	Pvt		John Durrmon Jr.
	PFC		Bernard B. Menies

Date	Rank	Killed in Action	Wounded in Action
	PFC		Lawrence A. Leohner
	Sgt		Frank A. Fulsom
	PFC		Lee A. Michwitz
	PFC		Jerry A. Stewart
	PFC		Morton L. Plesser
	PFC		Howard G. Johnson
	PFC		Edward C. Feanessey
Feb 1	T/Sgt		Lee J. Albers
	PFC		Raymond H. Locra
	PFC		Homer Mattos
Feb 2	Sgt	William G. Welch	
	PFC	William J. Evans	
Feb 3	S/Sgt		Orville A. Reagan
	Sgt		Ben M. Combs
	PFC		Harold J. Coultas
Feb 5	PFC		Victor A. Sayer
	PFC		Benny V. Tito
Feb 6	T/5		Edwin E. Dougherty
	PFC		Jerome Goldman
	PFC		Gladwin I. Maplethorpe
Feb 7	Pvt	James F. Reid	
	2LT		Richard Thompson
Feb 8	PFC		Dick. Forni
	PFC		Anthony McAwley
	T/Sgt		George G. Thompson
March 9	PFC	Frank Mora	
March 12	2LT	Clifford C. Seymour	

Date	Rank	Killed in Action	Wounded in Action
	Sgt	Cecil H. Brooks	
	PFC	Arthur F. Giustizia	
	Sgt		Uge F. Calcagno
	Pvt		Charles F. Claussen
March 26	PFC		James A. Kriz
	PFC		Marvin C. Turner
April 3	PFC		Jenniag M. Brown
	PFC		Donald F. Gresshans
April 4	T/Sgt		John P. Karlowski
	PFC		Cheslie M. Jones
	PFC		James F. Jones
	PFC		Robert C. Sterms
April 6	PFC	Odell T. Barbee	
	PFC	Edmund A. Bonadi	
	PFC	Charles W. Curtis	
	PFC	Gerald E. Dickinson	
	2LT		Felix W. Buchanan
	2LT		Richard J. Thompson
	S/Sgt		Delwyn P. Goodyear
	S/Sgt		Joseph R. Kirk
	S/Sgt		Charles A. Pippy
	S/Sgt		Elmer E. Prestridge
	T/5		Ignatius Crischun
	Cpl		Marvin G. Ryman
	T/4		Sydney K. Silverman
	PFC		Alfonso Bennett
	PFC		Verser R. Busic
	PFC		Laurence L. Gierach
	PFC		Raymond D. Jelle

Date	Rank	Killed in Action	Wounded in Action
April 7	2LT		Richard Thompson
	PFC		Bernard Jacobson
	PFC		William Kosika Jr.
	PFC		Beryl A. Lantz
	PFC		Ernest J. Siewert
	PFC		John M. Trejo
	PFC		Carey C. West
April 8	Sgt	Carl A. Randa	
April 12	Sgt	Francis W. Shea	
	PFC	Russell Cross	
	PFC	Kay D. Edge	
	PFC	William E. Ford	
	2LT		Robert J. Stegen
	T/4		Paul Winer
	PFC		Franklin Alcott
	PFC		Jesse H. Brenner
	PFC		Dale H. Brink
	PFC		Robert J. Eagle
	PFC		John T. Gavin
	PFC		Henry J. Gressler
	PFC		Troy W. Melton
	PFC		Edward Letourneau
	PFC		Phillip J. Romano

From 291st Infantry Regiment official action against enemy reports the following were awarded the Purple Heart Medal. So it must be assumed that they were wounded.

Dates not known	Sgt		Joseph Hessell Jr.
	Sgt		Douglas Huff
	T/Sgt		Irwin P. Chitwood
	T/Sgt		Cecil A. Helphinstine
	PFC		Richard H. Dietze
	PFC		Eugene V. Mendoza
	PFC		August E. Owens
	PFC		Ronald B. Collette
	S/Sgt		Nathan Henn
	Unk		Frank Fulsom

LT Hanser wrote Capt Sam Drake on April 18 1946 that Sgt. John P. Karlowski reported that the following casualties were suffered from 3rd Platoon but had not shown up on the official report.

Dates not known	Unk	Dodge	
Ranks unknown	Unk		Hutsen
	Unk		Boggess
	Unk		Ingeguatte
	Sgt		Shelton

In a letter dated 1-14-87, Dick Forni stated S/SGT Buchanan and Sgt Lamb and others were wounded during the Battle of the Bulge. Sgt Lamb was not on the list of WIA.[137]

A total of 26 Fox Company men were killed and 106 were wounded. There were 65 men during the Battle of the Bulge who were non battle casualties, mostly frostbite, frozen limbs, trench foot, cold sickness, etc. injury. After the war, at least one Fox veteran suffered from nerves, what doctors today would call post traumatic distress.

APPENDIX B

MEN WHO SERVED IN FOX COMPANY

PROBABLY CLOSE TO 400 men served in Fox Company, since it started the Bulge with 6 officers and 190 men. Fox returned to Holland after the Colmar Pocket it had 2 officers and 65 men. In Holland Fox was brought back up to 6 officers and 190 men. Some men were in the company for a very short and their names not recorded. Some chose not to attend reunions and little is known about their lives after the war. Many men are now dead and their personal information was not recorded, such as rank, platoon, or married. This list tries to show that most men married, raised families and got on with their lives after the war.

RANK, NAME, PLATOON/ POSITION, LIFE AFTER WAR

A

S/SGT Earl Adams Jr., Squad Leader 3rd Squad, 2nd Platoon, Married, three children. After College and ROTC went back in the Army as an officer. Retired in 1978 with 32 years of service as a Colonel. Served in Korea and Viet Nam

Sgt Walter Adamski Headquarters' section, personnel clerk

PFC Joe Affeldt, weapons platoon, Married one daughter, Security guard at Ansco and then GAF

T/Sgt Lee J. Albers, Weapons Platoon Sergeant, WIA

PFC Frank Alcott, Weapons platoon, WIA

PFC Roland Alexander

PFC Thomas Allin, 2nd platoon, Married, 2 daughters, Senior Trust Officer at Chase bank in the Personal Trust Department

T/5 Stanley Andy Anderson, Headquarters' section, Cooks Helper, married

PFC Hank Arend, Headquarters' section, Alternate Jeep Driver Married, 6 children, auto mechanic and owner of an auto repair shop

B

Pvt John Badgett, 3rd Squad, 2nd Platoon

PFC Raymond Bagley, 3rd Squad, 2nd Platoon, married five children, Farmer

Sgt Baker

PFC Odell T. Barbee, KIA

PFC Edward Baronian, Weapons Platoon

PFC Robert Bell

Pvt Robert D. Benish, 1st squad, 2nd Platoon, KIA, only child of parents from Milwaukee

PFC Earnest Benner

PFC Alfonso Bennett, WIA

S/Sgt Robert Berkebile, Squad leader 1st Squad, 2nd Platoon, WIA, Married, two daughters, Served as a Methodist Pastor for 36 years

PFC Buck Birmingham 3rd Platoon, snow blinded

PFC Delmar Black

Pvt Leroy Blankenbiller

PFC Robert Boggess 3rd Platoon, WIA

PFC Bomba 2nd Platoon

PFC Bowers

2LT Paul K. Bowman , Weapons Platoon Leader, KIA at Grand Halleux, an only child

PFC Jesse H. Brenner, 1st Platoon, WIA

PFC Franklin Brewer 3rd Platoon

PFC Dale H. Brink, WIA

PFC Edmund A. Bonadi, KIA

Sgt Cecil H. Brooks, Weapons Platoon, WIA

PFC Jennings M. Brown, 1st Platoon, WIA

PFC Kenneth Brown 3rd Platoon, Headquarters' section, Medic

T/Sgt Percy Brown 3rd Platoon, Platoon Sergeant

2LT Felix W. Buchanan, Weapons Platoon, WIA
S/Sgt Rupert K. Buchanen, Weapons Platoon, WIA
PFC Ellis Bull
PFC George Burgess
PFC Verser R. Busic, WIA

C

Sgt Uge F. Calcagno, WIA
LT Harvey Cannon, 2nd Platoon leader & later Commander of Company
    E, Stayed in the Army as a Transportation Officer and retired as a
    Lieutenant Colonel
Sgt Thomas Cardoza
PFC Maurice (Red) Carr, 3rd Squad, 2nd Platoon, Married, farm
    implement dealer, 4 children
PFC Angelo Cassarino
PFC Bob Chambers
PFC Carlos Chavez
T/Sgt & 2LT Irwin P. Chitwood, Platoon Sergeant and 3rd Platoon
    Leader, WIA, Married, 2 children, Retired from the Army as an
    E8 after 26 years of service.
PFC John Churas
PFC Cesidio Cipriani, Weapons Platoon, Married
Cpl Walter Clausius, 2nd Platoon, WIA
Pvt Charles F. Claussen, WIA
PFC Ronald B. Collette, 1st Squad, 2nd Platoon, WIA
Cpl Coleman Headquarters' section, Cmdr Bodyguard & Interpreter
    (spoke 6 foreign languages)
Sgt Ben M. Combs WIA, Weapons Platoon, Married, Judge
PFC Ernie Contreras
PFC Harold J. Coultas, Weapons Platoon, WIA
Capt Edgar (Ted) Cox, XO & Company Commander, Married, four
    children, Taught Agriculture, worked in real estate and sold farm
    equipment, esp. Kubota tractors.
PFC Albert Craig, married
PFC Allen W. Craig, WIA
T/5 Ignatius Crischun, WIA
PFC Russell Cross, 1st Platoon, KIA
PFC Richard Cummelin
PFC Charles W. Curtis, KIA

<u>D</u>

PFC James Floyd Davis 2nd Platoon, Married 4 children, farmer

PFC Ralph Davis

S/Sgt Richard DeBruyn, Squad Leader 1st Platoon, WIA, Married, letter carrier, Buffalo NY

1LT Lee Denton, HQ section, Company XO, recalled for the Korean War and was badly wounded in the leg

PFC Gerald E. Dickinson, Weapons Platoon, KIA

PFC Richard H. Dietze, WIA

PFC Richard Dixon Weapons Platoon

T/Sgt Oris Dobbins, Platoon Sergeant 2nd Platoon, Transferred out of company before Fox went overseas.

PFC Howard Dodge 3rd Platoon, WIA

T/5 Edwin E. Dougherty, WIA

Capt James (Sam) Drake, Company Commander, WIA, Married, 2 children, High School Football Coach

Capt Gene Droulliard, First Commander of Fox at Fort Leonard Wood, soon took Command of Company G and was wounded at Grand Halleux, Stayed in Army and retired as a Colonel

Pvt John Durrmon Jr., WIA

<u>E</u>

PFC Robert J. Eagle, WIA

T/4 Glen Eddington Hq section, Two and a half ton truck driver

Pvt Kay D. Edge, WIA and later KIA 1st platoon

Cpl Edmunson, HQ section Jeep Driver

PFC Royal Elf

PFC Ivan Else, 3rd Squad, 2nd Platoon

PFC John Ellis

PFC Kenneth Entler

PFC William J. Evans, KIA

PFC Earl Everett, 1st platoon, Married

PFC Wilber C. Evrard, WIA

<u>F</u>

PFC Edward C. Fennessey, WIA, Married one child, Deputy clerk, Mahoning County Probate Court

PFC John Fetrow Headquarters' section, Cooks Helper, Married, 2 children, Heavy duty truck mechanic

PFC John Fetson, Married

Sgt William Flenning, 2nd Platoon

Sgt Frank A. Folsom, 3rd Platoon, WIA

PFC Clyde Forehand, Weapons Platoon

PFC William E. Ford, 3rd Platoon, KIA

PFC and S/Sgt Emil 'Dick' Forni, Squad leader 1st Squad, 1st Platoon, WIA

PFC Lloyd Fowler Headquarters' section, Jeep Driver

PFC David Frazier, Weapons Platoon

Pvt Alfred S. Freeman, WIA

T/Sgt "Pappy" French, Platoon Sergeant, 2nd platoon

G

PFC John T. Gavin, WIA

Pvt John J. Gettuse, WIA

Sgt Joe Gibson, 3rd Platoon, Married, four Children, Republic Aviation[138]

PFC Laurence L. Giersche, WIA

PFC Arthur F. Giustizia, KIA

S/Sgt Donnie W. Glasscock, 3rd Platoon Squad Leader, KIA

PFC Harvey Glenn Jr. 1st Squad, 2nd Platoon

PFC Leon Gold

PFC Jerome Goldman WIA, 1st Platoon

S/Sgt Delwyn P. Goodyear, Squad Leader 2nd Squad, 2nd Platoon, WIA, Married, one son, High School teacher and Coach

Pvt Leonard Gordon

PFC Donald F. Gresshans, WIA

PFC Henry J. Gressler, WIA

Sgt George Grubbs HQ section, Cooks Helper

PFC Guistuzia, Weapons Platoon, KIA

H

PFC B. Haddox

Sgt James Hager

2LT William F. Hanser, 3rd Platoon, WIA, Married

PFC Grover E. Hardy, Headquarters' section, Cooks Helper, WIA

Sgt Gordon Harvey

PFC Bill Hayes, 2nd Platoon
T/Sgt Cecil A. Helphinstine, Weapons Platoon, WIA
S/Sgt Nathan Henn, Squad member and later Squad Leader, 1st Squad,
    2nd Platoon, Married
S/Sgt Kenneth Henson
Sgt Joseph Hessell Jr., Weapons Platoon, WIA
PFC Arthur Hiersche Married two children
T/5 Charles Holt HQ section, Cooks Helper
PFC Calvin W. Hood, WIA
PFC Jack R. Hudson, WIA
Sgt Douglas Huff, 3rd Squad, 2nd Platoon, WIA,Married
PFC John Hughes, 3rd Squad, 2nd Platoon, KIA
PFC Jack Hutson WIA, 3rd Platoon, WIA

I

PFC Ingeguatte, 3rd Platoon, WIA

J

PFC Bernard Jacobson, WIA
PFC Raymond D. Jelle, WIA
PFC Howard G. Johnson, 3rd Platoon, WIA
PFC DeWayne Johnson
S/Sgt Merle V. Johnson, 3rd Platoon Squad Leader, WIA,Married
PFC Cheslie M. Jones, WIA
PFC James F. Jones, WIA
LT Foster Jones, 2nd Platoon leader, Married, 3 children, District Manager
    of Haverty Furniture Company

K

PFC Frank Kantor
T/Sgt and later 1Sgt John F. Karlowski, 3rd Platoon, WIA
PFC Arthur Keinert
S/Sgt Russell L. Kime, 1st Platoon, Married , WIA
S/Sgt Joseph R. Kirk, Squad leader, 1st Squad, 2nd Platoon, WIA
PFC John H Klimek, 3rd Platoon,KIA, married before shipping out to
    Europe
PFC George Klochan 1st Platoon
PFC William Kosika Jr., WIA
PFC James A. Kriz, WIA

L

PFC Lachat
PFC Harry Ladenthin
Sgt Lamb WIA, 1st Platoon
PFC John Lamontia
PFC Beryl A. Lantz , 2nd Platoon, WIA,Married
PFC Paul Laskoski HQ section, personnel clerk
PFC Morris Latimer
PFC Lawrence Lechner, WIA
PFC John Leffler
PFC R.L. Lenox
PFC James Leonard
PFC Lawrence A Leohner
PFC Edward Letourneau, 3rd Platoon, WIA, Married, 7 children, 32 years as an IRS agent
PFC Charles Lewellen
PFC Carol Locket
PFC Thomas Lockwood
PFC Raymond H. Locra, WIA
PFC Arthur Long
PFC John L. Longo,3rd Squad, 2nd Platoon, WIA
PFC Bill Lowery

M

PFC John A. Mack, WIA
PFC William Maher, Married with children, Policeman at East Haven, CN
Cpl Dolor Mallette HQ section, 300 Radio Man
PFC Gladwin I. Maplethorpe, WIA
PFC Homer Martin
PFC Homer Mattos, WIA
PFC Mattice 1st Platoon
PFC Anthony McAwley, WIA
PFC Hugh McDermott, 3rd Platoon, KIA
PFC Wlliam McIlheney
S/SGT John McKay, Squad leader & Supply Sergeant, Married 5 children, Plumber,
PFC Paul McKee Headquarters' section, medic

PFC Ridley W. Meeks, KIA
PFC Troy W. Melton, WIA
PFC Edwin McMenemy, Weapons Platoon
PFC John Meisenback
PFC Eugene V. Mendoza, WIA
PFC Bernard B. Menies, WIA
PFC Lee A. Michwitz, WIA
Pvt Tom Milana
Sgt George Miller, HQ section, Supply Sergeant
PFC Charles Minarsich
PFC Ken Moody
PFC Daniel Mooney, 1st Squad, 2nd Platoon, WIA
PFC Frank Mora, KIA
S/Sgt Harold Moss 1st Platoon
Cpl Mumford, Headquarters' section, medic
PFC Edward Munic
PFC Lowell Murphy, 1st Squad, 2nd Platoon

N
S/Sgt Don Nadeau, HQ section, Mess Sgt, Married, one daughter, Assistant manger Grocery store and salesman for Sunshine Biscuits
PFC Bert W. Nelson, KIA
S/Sgt Ed Neville, Weapons Platoon, Mortar squad leader, Married, 3 children, Color Camera Foreman for RR Donnelly
PFC Eugene Noland

O
PFC Franklin Olcott
PFC Rudolph Olquin
PFC August E. Owens, WIA

P
PFC James Pagliarulo
PFC Emil Patrick
PFC Lewellyn Pannell
PFC Frederick Peterson
PFC Glenn Peterson, Weapons Platoon

PFC Dick Phillips, 3rd Squad, 2nd Platoon, Married, two children, Carpenter

PFC John Phillip HQ section, clerk

PFC Fred Pileski

S/Sgt Charles A. Pippy, Squad Leader 2nd Squad, 1st Platoon, WIA

PFC Morton L. Plesser, 3rd Squad, 2nd Platoon, WIA

S/Sgt Earnest Porter, Weapons Platoon, Mortar Section Sergeant

S/Sgt Elmer E. Prestridge Squad Leader, 3rd Squad, 1st Platoon

PFC Al Putnam, Weapons Platoon ,Married

Q

PFC Francis Quinn

R

PFC Robert Rader Jr. Married

PFC Otto Rainer

PFC Carl A. Randa, Weapons Platoon, KIA

PFC Donald Raver

S/Sgt Orville A. Reagan, 1st Platoon guide, WIA

PFC Jack Reese, 1st Squad, 2nd Platoon, Platoon sniper, Married, 7 children, Businessman

Pvt James F. Reid, KIA

PFC Fred Reither, 2nd Platoon, Married, 2 children, State Judge

PFC Everett Reynoso, 2nd Platoon

PFC Phillip J. Romano, WIA

PFC Thomas E. Royster, 3rd Squad, 2nd Platoon, WIA

PFC Milton Russen

Cpl Mervin G. Ryman, 2nd Platoon, WIA

S

PFC Victor A. Sayer, WIA

PFC Dick Scatena, HQ section, Mail Clerk, Married

PFC Buck Schaefer, 1st Squad, 2nd platoon

PFC Andrew Schaft

S/Sgt Pearson C. Schiller 2nd platoon guide

PFC George Schmalbeck,

PFC Walter Setters

2LT Clifford C. Seymour 3rd Platoon Leader, KIA

PFC Fred Shank, 1st Squad, 2nd Platoon

Pvt Alexander F. Shannon, WIA

S/Sgt Francis W. Shea, 3rd Platoon Squad Leader, KIA

S/Sgt Clarence Shelton 3rd Platoon, Platoon guide, WIA

PFC RW Short

PFC Clarence Shorter

PFC Dick Siakel, 1st Squad, 2nd Platoon, Married, 2 children, Commercial Photographer

PFC Ernest J. Siewert, WIA

1Sgt David Sigmund

T/4 Sydney K. Silverman, WIA

PFC Singer, Harry 3rd Squad, 2nd Platoon

PFC Jack Smith

PFC Samuel Smith, 1st Squad, 2nd Platoon

PFC Truman Smith

PFC Robert Solomon

PFC Dale Speak

PFC Thomas Stackhouse

PFC Howard Statham

2LT Robert J. Stegen, 1st Platoon Leader, WIA, Married, 3 children, Worked 37 years as a Department of the Army civilian in Supply

PFC Robert C. Sterms, WIA

Pvt Jerry Steward, 3rd Squad, 2nd Platoon

PFC Jerry A. Stewert 2nd Platoon, WIA

Cpl Ray Stoddard, 1st platoon & HQ section, 300 Radio Man & Company Sniper, Married, 3 daughters, Worked at Twin City Arsenal, Owned Publisher's Representative Business DBA Company, as of 2011 still working delivering new cars to car dealerships.

PFC Guy Stone

PFC Robert Storms

PFC William Swzackowski

T

PFC John Tarasevich , Married

PFC Thomas Taylor Jr, 1st Platoon, Married 2 children, Police Detective for Washington DC

PFC J. Techner

PFC Walter K. Thabit, WIA

PFC Richard J. Thibault, WIA

T/Sgt George Thomas, 1st Platoon Sergeant

PFC Robert Thomas
T/Sgt George G. Thompson, WIA
2LT Richard J. Thompson, WIA
PFC Benny V. Tito, 1ˢᵗ Platoon, WIA
PFC Edward Toppino
PFC John M. Trejo, WIA
PFC Charles Tuhacek
PFC Marvin C. Turner, WIA
PFC Edward Tweedle HQ section, Company Barber & other assigned
    duties

V
PFC Fred Valet

W
PFC Wagner 1ˢᵗ Platoon
Sgt Robert Wallace 1ˢᵗ Platoon
T/5 Red Watland, 1ˢᵗ Squad, 2ⁿᵈ Platoon
PFC Lyle H. Watts, WIA
PFC Carey West
PFC Robert E. West Jr
PFC Robert V. West 2ⁿᵈ Platoon
Sgt William G. Welch, 3ʳᵈ Platoon, KIA
PFC Carey C. West, WIA
PFC Forrest Wethington
PFC Frank Wheelus
PFC Rex A. Williams, WIA
PFC Arthur Wilsey
PFC James S. Winebrenner, Weapons Platoon, KIA
T/4 Paul Winer, WIA
PFC George Wingard
T/5 John Winters HQ section, Armor Artificer
PFC Wise 1ˢᵗ platoon
PFC Sammie Woodruff
PFC Murray Wolpert, 2ⁿᵈ platoon
PFC William Wright Headquarters' section, clerk

APPENDIX C

★ ★ ★

PORTRAITS OF MEN OF FOX

S/Sgt Earl Adams, 1943. 20 year old Squad Leader, 2nd Platoon
Typical of how young the Fox Company men were

PFC Joe Affeldt, Weapons Platoon

Photo from Clemson Alumni Association
2LT Paul K Bowman, Weapons Platoon Leader, PK was the
first member of Fox to be killed, 1-15-45 at Grand Halleaux. He
was from Dalzell, SC a small farming community. He attended
Clemson University for 3 years as a Chemistry major. He was
an only son, whose parents were crushed by his death.[139]

Red Carr joined Fox Company in Holland. He was called Red because of his red hair. He was assigned to 3rd Squad 2nd Platoon where he made a life long friendship with Dick Phillips

Ted Cox as a 2ⁿᵈ Lieutenant, Served as Company
Executive Officer and Company Commander

Portrait of PFC Richard Phillips

PFC John Fetrow, Cook's helper

PFC Ed Letourneau, 3rd Platoon. Wounded on last day of combat April 12th 1945.

*Ed Letourneau and friend, probably a studio picture made in Paris
Fox men liked to go to Paris with Ed since he spoke French.*

Ed Neville, Mortar Squad leader, Weapons Platoon

PFC Everett Reynoso 2nd Platoon

Corporal Ray Stoddard, Headquarter section, radio man and jeep driver.

APPENDIX D

✳ ✳ ✳

STEGEN'S LIST LOCATIONS

2LT Bob Stegen Platoon leader of 1st Platoon lists reference points and dates as he recalled the actions of Fox Company Attacking from Holland into Germany.[140]

1.	Feb 20	Haelen-Buggennumn, Holland
2.	March 3	Veldem-Lomn, Holland
3.	March 4	Arcen, Holland
4.	March 5&6	Geldern, Germany
5.	March 7-26	Milchplatz, Germany
6.	March 28	Dorsten, Germany attacked 5:30 am
7.	March 28	Marl, Germany Released slave labors at synthetic Rubber Plant
8.	March 29	Sickingmuhle, Germany fought house to house
9.	March 30&31	Die Haard Forest & Flaesheum 1st platoon on tanks
10.	April 1 thru 4	Datteln rest
11.	April 6 thru 9	Rutgers Castle and surrounding area tough few days
12.	April 10	Lutgen Dortmund, 1st platoon advance party to relieve 289th Infantry
13.	April 11	Eichlinghofen & Meglinghausen Fire fight at first named town and took second named town at night
14.	April 12	1st platoon at Persebeck LT Stegen wounded

APPENDIX E

★ ★ ★

BELGIAN AWARD

DEPARTMENT OF THE ARMY
Washington 25, D.C., 10 December 47

GENERAL ORDERS }
No. 24 }

UNITS ENTITLED TO FOREIGN DECORATIONS

Section

GENERAL _____ I
LIST OF UNITS AND CITATIONS _____ II

I.—GENERAL.—1. The following list of units of the United States Army to which decorations have been awarded by cobelligerent foreign governments during World War II, together with the citations therefor, is confirmed, in accordance with paragraph 2, AR 260-15.

2. Individual wear of the French and Belgium Fourrageres and the Netherlands Orange Lanyard will be in accordance with the provisions of paragraph 18, AR 260-15.

BELGIAN CROIX DE GUERRE, awarded under Decree No. 514, 22 May 1945, as amended by Decree No. 3864, 28 April 1947, by Charles, Prince of Belgium, Regent of the Kingdom, with the following citation:

During the German offensive in the Ardennes, in December 1944, the 2d Armored Division was located in Germany, on the banks of the Roer River between Linnich and Julich. On 21 December 1944, it received orders to proceed to the region of Havelange, Avin Clavier. This movement of more than 100 miles was accomplished in less than 24 hours and on 23 December 1944, the Division established contact with hostile forces at Celles. From the 23d to the 28th of December 1944, violent engagements developed in the Celles salient and brought about the total destruction of the spearhead division of the Fifth Panzer Army. This victory blocked the German advance and prevented it from reaching the Meuse. From thence on, the Division pushed back the enemy forces and, after having retaken many communities of the Ardennes region, it liberated the town of Houffalize.

BELGIAN FOURRAGERE (1940), awarded under Decree No. 514, 22 May 1945, as amended by Decree No. 3864, 28 April 1947, by Charles, Prince of Belgium, Regent of the Kingdom.

75TH INFANTRY DIVISION

291st Inf Regiment, 2 Bn (Atchd to 2d Armd Div)
BELGIAN CROIX DE GUERRE, awarded under Decree No. 3864, 28 April 1947, by

APPENDIX F

★ ★ ★

REUNIONS

TED COX KEPT RECORDS of the men who served in Fox Company and organized reunions that kept Fox Company together. Some Company reunions were held around the country where the 75th Division Veterans association held their reunion. Other times, Ted would organize a reunion in his home town of Saint Charles, MO. In the 1980's about 30 men would attend the reunions. From interviews with widows, it was stated the veterans found the reunion therapeutic, where they could talk about the war. Some men corresponded with Ted Cox but did not come to reunions. Some probably wanted to forget the war. Others could not get away from work. For example, James Davis never came because he had a small farm that he could not leave, where he raised 4 children. His son Bill later joined as a Fox Company as an associate member and attended about 5 reunions. Over time deaths and health problems reduced the number who could make it to a reunion.

Left to Right: Cesidio Cipriane, Colonel Jesse Drain, Captain Sam Drake
1971 Reunion at Indianapolis

July 1990 Reunion in Saint Charles, Mo
Front row L to R: Bob Stegen, Ted Cox; 2ⁿᵈ row L to R: Beryl Lantz, Doug Huff, Fred Reither, Sam Drake, John Tarasevich, Ben Combs, Dick Siakel, Carey West Back Row L to R: Ray Stoddard, Ed Fenessey, Foster Jones, John Fetrow , Buck Schaefer, Harvey Cannon, Carey West, Earl Adams, Dick Phillips, Irwin Chitwood (back), Dick Scatena, Jack McKay (back) Hank Arend

July 1990, Dick Phillips, Doug Huff, Earl Adams: members of 3rd Squad, 2nd Platoon The American Flag in the background flew over Fox Company's Command Post at the end of the war and was kept by Ted Cox as a treasured memento.

1991 LT R Dick Scatena, Sam Drake, Jack McKay, Hank Arend, Bob Stegen, Earl Adams, Foster Jones, Ben Combs, Del Goodyear

Reunion 1991 at Earl Adams house in Everett, WA
Knelling left to right: Hank & Jean Arend, John Tarasevich,
Marine & Dick Scatena
Standing Ladies: Mary Cox, Ann Combs, Justine Stegen,
Mary Lee Adams, Dot Tarasevich, Thelma Fetrow,
Nena Jones, Lorraine McKay, Elaine Goodyear, Mary Drake
Standing Men: Ted Cox, Ben Combs, Bob Stegen, Earl Adams, John
Fetrow, Foster Jones, Jack McKay, Del Goodyear, Sam Drake

Reunion July 1992 at John Fetrow's house Valley Forge, PA
Back row L to R Dick Scatena, Ted Cox, Sam Drake, Jack McKay, Thomas Allin, Virginia Allin, John Fetrow, Doug Huff, Dick Phillips, George Schmalbeck, Beryl Lantz
Seated: Maxine Scatena, Thelma Fetrow, Mary Drake, Mary Cox, Lorraine McKay, Geneva Huff, Bonnie Phillips, Betty Schmalbeck , June Lantz

Ted Cox, John Fetrow, Gene Droulliard, Sam Drake 1992
Cox, Drulliard and Drake commanded Fox Company. Drake was wounded
during the attack at Aldringen. Drulliard was the first commander of Fox
and then was transferred to Company G and was wounded during the
attack from Grand Halleux. Drulliard appointed several men, such as
Adams, Goodyear, and Berkebile corporals after the first initial training.

York, PA, July 20, 1992 Fox Reunion
*Front row: Dick Phillips, Sam Drake, John Fetrow,
John Tarasevich, Ted Cox
Middle row: Beryl Lantz, Doug Huff, Ed Fennessey, Dick Scatena
Back row: Albert Craig, Ben Combs, Jack McKay,
Thomas Allin, Foster Jones, George Schmalbeck*

Reunion at West Point, NY, September 8, 1993
Front: John Tarasevich, Sam Drake, Bob Berkebile, John Fetrow
Back: Ted Cox, Joe Affeldt, Albert Craig, Foster Jones

Sam and Mary Drake 1993. Sam trained Fox Company and commanded until wounded in the Battle of the Bulge

Ray Bagley and Dick Phillips July 1993 at Ray's Missouri Farm

Red Carr and Dick Phillips July 1993 at Red's Nebraska home

Tom Taylor and Ray Stoddard

Edgar "Ted" Cox and Scott Adams

Front Row left to right: Doug Huff, John Fetrow, Foster Jones
Back row: Ted Cox, Al Craig, Bob Stegen, Jack McKay

Reunion 2003 Front row: McKay, Cox, Reither
Back row: Davis, Phillips, Stegen, Fetrow, Siakel, Stoddard, Chitwood

The ten men who attended 2006 reunion
Front Row Fetrow, Cox, Stoddard, Chitwood
Back row: Stegen, Reither, Craig, Davis, Siakel, Putnam

APPENDIX G

★ ★ ★

CAMPAIGN MAPS

THE NEXT THREE MAPS were made by the G3 section of the 75ᵗʰ Infantry Division for the pamphlet "The 75ᵗʰ Infantry Division in Combat" printed at Camp Baltimore.

Map of the Battle of Battle in the Ardennes[141]

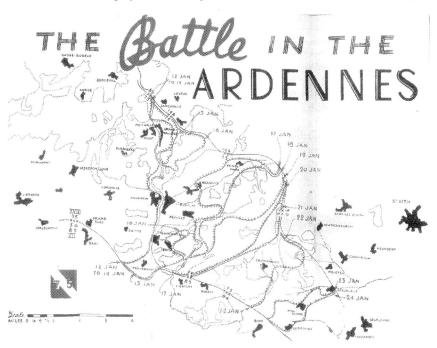

Map of the Colmar Pocket[142]

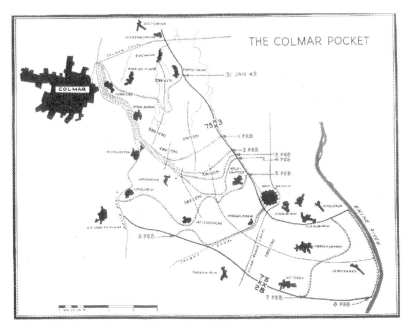

Map of the Battle for the Ruhr[143]

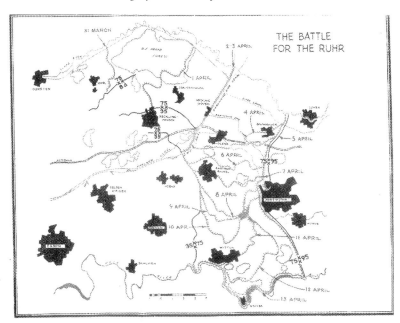

WORKS CITED

✶ ✶ ✶

1. Adams, Earl, "Letter to Aunt and Uncle Fosse" dated November 24, 1944.
2. Adams, Earl, "Letter to Aunt and Uncle Fosse" dated July 19, 1944
3. Adams, Earl, "letter to Aunt and Uncle Fosse", January 8, 1945.
4. Adams, Earl, "Letter to Aunt and Uncle Fosse", postmarked April 12, 1945.
5. Alexander, Larry, *The Biggest Brother, The life of Major Dick Winters, The Man who led the band of Brothers*, New York, NAL Caliber, 2005.
6. Allen, Tonya, "The sinking of SS Leopoldville", www.uboat.net?history/Leopoldville.htm.
7. "Allied Forces slice miles from Bulge", Stars and Stripes, Volume 1 number 171, dated 14 Jan. 1945.
8. Ambrose, Stephen, *Citizen Soldiers*, New York, New York, Simon and Schuster, 1997.
9. Ambrose, Stephen, *D-Day*, New York, New York, Simon and Schuster, 1994.
10. Arend, Geoff, email sending photos dated May 1, 2011
11. Stars & Stripes, *The 75ᵗʰ*, Paris, 1945.
12. "Battle of Okinawa", Wikipedia, http://en.wikipedia.org/wiki/Battle_of_okinawa, 2011.
13. Bell, Jack, "Poorly clothed Yanks freezing on West Front, Writer charges", Minneapolis Star Journal and Chicago Daily News 26 January 1945.

14. Bowman, Paul, Clemson Alumni Association, http://cualumni.clemson.edu/page.aspx?pid=1453.

15. Berkebile, Bob letter to Scott Adams, dated August 13, 2006

16. Berkebile, Bob, letter to Scott Adams, dated October 16, 2007

17. Berkebile, Bob, letter to Scott Adams, dated January, 19, 2011.

18. *The Bulge Buster*, Number 1 Volume 1, May 1946.

19. Bradley, Omar and Clay Blair, *A General's Life*, Simon and Schuster, New York, 1983.

20. Bradley, Omar, *A soldier's story*, Holt, New York, 1951.

21. Carr, Larry, Email to Scott Adams, dated January 23,2012

22. Coggins, David, *75th Infantry Division*, Turner Publishing, Paducah, Kentucky, 1999.

23. Cox, Edgar, written memories of World War 2. dated, 9 July, 2010.

24. Cox, Edgar, written memories of World War 2. dated, 24 February, 2011

25. Cox, Edgar, F Company 291st Infantry roster, dated 15 May, 1971.

26. Cox, Edgar, List of members of F Company killed and wounded in action during World War 2, undated.

27. Cox, Edgar, Lists of members of F Company awarded the Good Conduct Medal, typed from list dated 19 September 1944.

28. Cox, Edgar, Lists of members of F Company awarded the Good Conduct Medal, typed from list dated 29 February, 1945.

29. Cox, Edgar, List of members of F Company awarded Expert Infantryman Badge, dated 15 July , 1944

30. DeBruyn, Richard, "Eye witness account during Battle of the Bulge", Special Winter supplement to the Guidon, Vol.VI, Number 1, February 1987.

31. DeBruyn, Richard, "Fearful Frosty, Freezing, and Frigid Flashbacks, The Guidon, undated.

32. Dounis, Peter, "The battle of Grand Halleux, The Bulge Buster, February, 1996.

33. Drake, Sam, "2ⁿᵈ Battalion Attacks" , The Bulge Buster, undated.

34. Drake, Sam, "Poteau", The Bulge Buster, undated.

35. Dupuy, Trevor, David Bongard, Richard Anderson, *Hitler's Last Gamble The Battle of the Bulge December 1944 January 1945*, New York, Harper Collins, 1994.

36. Fetrow, John, letter to Scott Adams, undated

37. Fetrow, John, letter to Scott Adams, dated January 27, 2011

38. Fetrow, John, letter to Scott Adams, dated February 28, 2011

39. Fetrow, John, letter to Scott Adams, dated March 16, 2011

40. Forni, Dick, Letter to Sam Drake, dated January, 1987, dated 14 January 1987.

41. Fort Leonard Wood News, VIII (39), "Post is Three Years Old, Ground Broken December 3, 1940", 3 December 1943.

42. Gazda, Tom, email to Scott Adams, dated April 22,2011

43. Gollan, Jennifer, "Lost and found: World War II memory", Marin Independent Journal, http://www.marinij.com/Sories/0,1413,234-24407-1901220,00.html.

44. Google map of Vielsalm, Belgium, Google, 2011.

45. Google map of Colmar , France, Google, 2011.

46. Google map of Dorsten, Germany, Google, 2011.

47. Google map of Castrop-Rauxel, Germany, Google 2011.

48. Google map of Persebeck, Germany, Google, 2011.

49. Hayes, Bill, Letter to Fred Reither, dated 20 May 1991.

50. Henn, Nathan, written memories of World War 2, undated

51. Honor Flight Network, www.honorflight.org.

52. Huston, James, *Biography of a Battalion*, Stackpole Books, Mechanicsburg, PA, 2003.

53. Jones, Russell, "1ˢᵗ and 75ᵗʰ cut two key roads", Stars and Stripes, 25 Jan. 1945, Volume 1, Number 6.

54. Korando, Russell, "We're like brothers'", Saint Charles Journal, 20 Sept. 2006.

55. Krosin, Richard, Interviews of Fox veterans, email April 6, 2011.

56. Letourneau, Ed, TV 6 Greenfield, Leon Weeks interview on Ed's memories of the World War 2, June 21 2000.

57. *The Mule*, Vol I (6), "Division Winds up Defensive Operations: On Offensive next 4 problems: 2 River Crossings, pages 1 and 3.

58. Nadeau, Don, phone conversation with Scott Adams, February 20, 2011.

59. Neville, Ed Written memories of World War2, undated.

60. Neville, Ed, Written Memories of World War 2, undated.

61. 106th Infantry Division (United States), http://en.wikipedia.org?wiki/106th_Infantry_Division_(United_States).

62. Powers, Rod, "Bronze Star Medal", http://usmilitary.about.com/od/armymedals/ss/bsm_4.htm.

63. Phillips, Dick, letter to Scott Adams, dated August 12, 2006.

64. Phillips, Dick, letter to Scott Adams, dated July 7, 2010.

65. Phillips, Sherry, email to Scott Adams, dated April 9, 2011.

66. Reese, Jack, written memories of World War 2, The Bulge Buster, undated.

67. *Register of Graduates and Former Cadets*, Bicentennial edition, The Association of Graduates, 2002.

68. Reither, Fred, written memories of World War 2, 26 January 1945.

69. Robert J. Dole Archives, "Robert J. Dole Timeline of Events", http://dolearchive.ku.edu/collections/archives/house/timeline.shtml.

70. "Route of the fighting 75th Division", The Bulge Buster, Vol. 1 No. 1, May 1946.

71. " Season's first cage champs", *The Mule*, clipping from 75th Infantry Division Newspaper, Fall 1945.

72. 75th Battle Command Training Division, http://www.usar.army.mil/arweb/organization/commandstructure/USARC/TNG/75BCTD/History/pages/default.aspx.

73. 75th Infantry Division (United States), http://en.wikipedia.org?wiki/75th_Infantry_Division_(United_States).

74. 75th Infantry Division G3 Staff, *The 75th Infantry Division in Combat*, Camp Baltimore France, 1944.

75. 75th Infantry Division Staff, *The 75th Infantry Division Pictorial History*, Atlanta, Albert Love Enterprises, 1944.

76. Siakel, Dick, phone conversation with Scott Adams, August 1, 2011.

77. 66th Infantry Division (United States), http://en.wikipedia.org/wiki/66th_Infantry_Division_(United States).

78. "SS Empire Javelin", Wikipedia, en.wikipedea.org/wiki/SS Empire Javelin.

79. 291ST Infantry Regiment Staff, "Actions against enemy report for December 1944, 291st Infantry Regiment, dated 6 February 1945.

80. 291ST Infantry Regiment Staff, "Actions against enemy report for January 1945, 291st Infantry Regiment, dated 6 February 1945.

81. 291ST Infantry Regiment Staff , "Actions against enemy report for February 1945, 291st Infantry Regiment, dated 2 March 1945.

82. 291ST Infantry Regiment Staff, "Actions against enemy report for March 1945, 291st Infantry Regiment, dated 2 April 1945.

83. 291ST Infantry Regiment Staff, "Actions against enemy report for April 1945, 291st Infantry Regiment, dated 2 May 1945.

84. 291st Infantry Regiment Staff, *Combat Diary of the 291st Infantry Regiment*, undated.

85. 291st Infantry Regiment Staff, "History of the 291st Infantry Regiment, undated.

86. Siakel, Dick, Phone conversation with Scott Adams, August 1, 2011

87. Stars & Stripes, *The 75th*, Paris, 1945.

88. Stegen, Bob, Lists of Towns he was in during World War 2, undated.

89. Stegen, Bob, phone conversation with Scott Adams, August 1, 2011.

90. Stoddard, Ray, Written overview of service in World War 2, undated.

91. Stoddard, Ray, Email to Scott Adams, February, 2, 2011

92. Stoddard, Ray, Email to Scott Adams, February, 4, 2011

93. Stoddard, Ray, Email to Scott Adams, February 23, 2011

94. Stoddard, Ray, Email to Scott Adams, October 27, 2011.

95. Stoddard, Ray, Email to Scott Adams, November 2, 2011.

96. Stoddard, Ray, Letter to Scott Adams, dated November 19, 2011.

97. Stoddard, Ray, written memories of the Battle of the Bulge, undated.

98. Stoddard, Ray, written memories of the Battle of the Bulge and Colmar Pocket, undated.

99. Stoddard, Ray, written memories of World War 2 after Colmar Pocket, undated.

100. *The Mule*, Vol I (6), "Division Winds up Defensive Operations: On Offensive next 4 problems: 2 River Crossings, pages 1 and 3.

101. "The U.S. 75th Infantry Division", http://steve-devault.suite101. com/the-us-75th-infantry-division-a21647.

102. "Walter Model" wikipdeia, en.wikipedia.org/wiki/Walter Model.

103. Wolf, Edward, Letter to the Editor, Newspaper unknown, date unknown, clipping from collection of Ted Cox.

104. Woolner, Franck, "Joes who know 'em say they're not", Stars and Stripes, 28 Jan. 1945, Vol. 1 No. 185.

105. Wuebben, Linda, "Crofton man 'finally' receives Bronze Star", Newspaper unknown, date unknown.

106. "Yanks gain 5 miles on Luzon Plain", The Stars and Stripes, Volume 1 Number 6, January 25, 1945.

107. Zraunig, Leslie, phone conversation with Ed Letourneau's daughter Leslie, May 21, 2011.

END NOTES

* * *

1. Stars and Stripes, The 75th, Paris, 1946, page 21.
2. Ambrose, Stephen, D-Day, New York New York, Simon and Schuster, 1994, page 48.
3. Fort Leonard Wood News, Vol III (39), "Post is three years old: Ground broken December 3 1940, page 1
4. 291st Infantry Regimental staff, "History of 291st Infantry Regiment", US Army Document, date unknown, pages 1- 7
5. Robert J. Dole Archives, "Robert J. Dole Timeline of Events", http://dolearchive.ku.edu/collections/archives/house/timeline.shtml.
6. Register of Graduates and Former Cadets, Bicentennial edition, The Association of Graduates, 2002, page 10626.
7. Huston, James, Biography of a Battalion, Stackpole Books, Mechanicsburg, PA, 2003, pages 15 to 16.
8. The Mule, Vol I (60, "Division Winds up Defensive Operations, On offensive next 4 problems; 2 River Crossings", pages 1 and 3.
9. Adams, Earl, "Letter to Aunt and Uncle Fosse from Camp Breckinridge" dated July 19, 1944, page 4.
10. 75th Infantry Division Staff, 75th Infantry Division, Pictorial History, Atlanta, Albert Love Enterprises. 1944, page 57.
11. Phillips, Dick, letter to Scott Adams, dated August 12, 2006, page 1.
12. "66th Infantry Division (United States)", Wikipedia, http://en.wikipedia.org/wiki/66th_Infantry_Division_(United States).

13. "SS Empire Javelin", Wikipedia, http://en.wikipedia.org/wiki/ SSEmpireJavelin.
14. Wolf, Edward, Letter to Editor, Unknown Florida Newspaper near Clear Water, FL. Dated unknown, page unknown.
15. Dupuy, Trevor, Hitler's Last Gamble, The Battle of the Bulge, New York, Harper Collins, 1994, pages 9-10.
16. Nadeau, Donald, Phone conversation with Scott Adams, February 20, 2011.
17. Stoddard, Ray, "My recollections as a foot soldier during January 1945, undated, page 1.
18. Dupuy, Trevor, Hitler's Last Gamble, The Battle of the Bulge, New York, Harper Collins, 1994 pages 324 – 325.
19. "Allied Forces slice miles from Bulge", Stars and Stripes, 14 January, 1945, page 1.
20. Google map of Vielsalm, Belgium, Google 2011.
21. Drake, Sam, "2nd Battalion attacks", The Bulge Buster, undated, page 7.
22. 291st Infantry Regiment Staff, "Actions Against the Enemy report for January 1945, appendix 1 page 6.
23. Dounis, Peter, "The Battle of Grand Halleux", The Bulge Buster, undated, page unknown.
24. Bell, Jack, "Poorly clothed Yanks freezing on West Front Writers Charges", Minneapolis Star Journal and Chicago Daily News, 26 January 1945, page unknown.
25. Berkebile, Bob, letter to Scott Adams, dated January 19, 2011.
26. Stoddard, Ray, "My recollections as a foot soldier during January 1945, pages 2-3
27. DeBruyn, Richard, "F-291 at Grand Halleux", Eye witness account during Battle of the Bulge, Special Winter supplement to the Guidon, Volume VI, Number 1, February 1996, page 1
28. Dupuy, Trevor, Hitler's Last Gamble, The Battle of the Bulge", New York, Harper Collins, 1994, page 325.
29. Drake, Sam, "Poteau", Bulge Buster, clipping undated, page unknown.
30. Letourneau, Ed, TV6 Greenfield MA, Interview on Ed's memories of World War 2. Video tape

31. DeBruyn, Richard, "Lost Patrol", An eye-witness account during the Battle of the Bulge, Special Winter supplement to the Guidon, Volume 1 Number 1 February 1987, pages 1-2.

32. DeBruyn, Richard, "Incident at Patteauxl", An eye-witness account during the Battle of the Bulge, Special Winter supplement to the Guidon, Volume 1 Number 1 February 1987, page 2.

33. Coggins, David, 75th Infantry Division, Turner Publishing, Paducah, Kentucky, 1999, page 26.

34. DeBruyn, Richard, "Incident at Patteauxl", An eye-witness account during the Battle of the Bulge, Special Winter supplement to the Guidon, Volume 1 Number 1 February 1987, page 3

35. DeBruyn, Richard, "Incident at Patteauxl", An eye-witness account during the Battle of the Bulge, Special Winter supplement to the Guidon, Volume 1 Number 1 February 1987, page 3-4.

36. Jones, Russell, "1st and 75th cut two key roads", The Stars and Stripes, Volume 1 number 6, January 25, 1945 pages 1 and 4.

37. "Yanks gain 5 miles on Luzon Plains" The Stars and Stripes, Volume 1 number 6, January 25, 1945 page 4.

38. Berkebile, Robert, Letter to Scott Adams, dated August 13, 2006, page 1-2.

39. Gollan, Jennifer, "Lost and found: World War II memory", Marin Independent Journal, http://www.marinij.com/Stories/0,1413,234~24407~1901220,00.html.

40. Adams, Earl, "Letter to Aunt and Uncle Fosse, post marked April 12, 1945, page 1.

41. Stoddard, Ray, Email to Scott Adams, dated February 4, 2011, pages 1-2.

42. Bradley, Omar, A General's Life, Simon and Schuster, New York, 1983, pages 387 to 389.

43. Koenigsdorf, R.H., "Actions against the enemy for the month of December 1944, 291st Infantry Regiment, dated 3 February 1945.

44. Koenigsdorf, R.H., "Actions against the enemy for the month of February 1945, 291st Infantry Regiment, dated 2 March 1945.

45. Krosin, Richard, interview of Fox veterans, email April 6, 2011.
46. Carey, Randolph, William Fox, David Hamlin, James Marion, Combat Diary of the 291ˢᵗ Infantry Regiment, undated.
47. Letourneau, Ed, "TV 6 Greenfield interview", dated June 21, 2000.
48. Google map of Colmar, France, Google 2011.
49. Woolner, Franck, "Joe's who know 'em say they're not", The Stars and Stripes, Volume 1 number 185, dated January 28, 1945, page 4.
50. 291ˢᵗ Infantry Regiment Staff, Overlay dated 1 February 1945, "Actions against the enemy report for February 1945", 291ˢᵗ Infantry Regiment, dated 2 March 1945.
51. 291ˢᵗ infantry Regiment staff, Overlay dated 5 February 1945, "Actions against the enemy report for February 1945", 291ˢᵗ Infantry Regiment, dated 2 March 1945.
52. Forni, Dick, Letter to Sam Drake, dated January, 1987, pages 1-2.
53. Stoddard, Ray, Written memories of the Battle of the Bulge and Colmar Pocket, undated pages 1-3.
54. Nadeau, Don, phone conversation with Scott Adams, February 20, 2011.
55. Stoddard, Ray, Written memories of the Battle of the Bulge and Colmar Pocket, undated page 3.
56. 291ˢᵗ Infantry Regiment Staff, "Actions against the enemy report for February 1945", 291ˢᵗ Infantry Regiment, dated 2 March 1945, page 2.
57. 291ˢᵗ Infantry Regiment Staff, "Actions against the enemy report for February 1945", 291ˢᵗ Infantry Regiment, dated 2 March 1945, page 5.
58. 291ˢᵗ Infantry Regiment Staff, Ovelay dated 21 February 1945, "Actions against the enemy report for February 1945", 291ˢᵗ Infantry Regiment, dated 2 March 1945.
59. 291ˢᵗ Infantry Regiment Staff, "Actions against the enemy report for February 1945", 291ˢᵗ Infantry Regiment, dated 2 March 1945, pages 5-6.
60. Bradley, Omar, A soldier's story, Holt, New York, 1951, pages 444 to 446.

61. Siakel, Dick, phone conservation with Scott Adams, August 1, 2011.

62. 291st Infantry Regiment Staff, Overlay dated 20 February 1945, "Actions against the enemy report for February 1945", 291st Infantry Regiment, dated 2 March 1945.

63. 291st Infantry Regiment Staff, Overlay dated 21 February 1945, "Actions against the enemy report for February 1945", 291st Infantry Regiment, dated 2 March 1945.

64. 291st Infantry Regiment Staff, Overlay dated 20 February 1945, "Actions against the enemy report for February 1945", 291st Infantry Regiment, dated 2 March 1945.

65. 291st Infantry Regiment Staff, Overlay dated 21 February 1945, "Actions against the enemy report for February 1945", 291st Infantry Regiment, dated 2 March 1945.

66. Forni, Dick, Letter to Sam Drake, dated January, 1987, page 3.

67. Stoddard, Ray, Written memories of World War 2 after Colmar Pocket, undated, page 1.

68. Nadeau, Don, phone conversation with Scott Adams, February 20, 2011.

69. Siakel, Dick, phone conversation with Scott Adams, August 1, 2011

70. 291st Infantry Regiment Staff, Narrative, "Actions against the enemy report for February 1945", 291st Infantry Regiment, dated 2 March 1945, pages 1-2.

71. Reither, Fred, "Written memories of World War 2", dated 26 January 1945, page 3.

72. 291st Infantry Regiment Staff, Narrative, "Actions against the enemy report for February 1945", 291st Infantry Regiment, dated 2 March 1945, page 2.

73. Siakel, Dick, phone conservation with Scott Adams, August 1, 2011.

74. Siakel, Dick, Phone conservation with Scott Adams, August 1, 2011.

75. 291st Infantry Regiment Staff, S3 Journal, Narrative, "Actions against the enemy report for February 1945", 291st Infantry Regiment, dated 2 March 1945, page 14.

76. 291ˢᵗ Infantry Regiment Staff, Narrative, "Actions against the enemy report for February 1945", 291ˢᵗ Infantry Regiment, dated 2 March 1945, pages 2-3.

77. 291ˢᵗ Infantry Regiment Staff, S3 Journal, Narrative, "Actions against the enemy report for February 1945", 291ˢᵗ Infantry Regiment, dated 2 March 1945, page 18.

78. Forni, Dick, Letter to Sam Drake, dated January, 1987, page 3.

79. Siakel, Dick, Phone conservation with Scott Adams, August 1, 2011.

80. Stoddard, Ray, Written memories of World War 2 after Colmar Pocket, undated, page 1.

81. Gazda, Tom, Email to Scott Adams, dated April 22, 2011.

82. 291ˢᵗ Infantry Regiment Staff, "Actions against the enemy report for February 1945", 291ˢᵗ Infantry Regiment, dated 2 March 1945, page 3.

83. Stoddard, Ray, Written memories of World War 2 after Colmar Pocket, undated, page 2.

84. 291ˢᵗ Infantry Regiment Staff, Overlay dated 26 March 1945, "Actions against the enemy report for February 1945", 291ˢᵗ Infantry Regiment, dated 2 March 1945.

85. 291ˢᵗ Infantry Regiment Staff, S3 Journal pages 26 -27, "Actions against the enemy report for February 1945", 291ˢᵗ Infantry Regiment, dated 2 March 1945.

86. 75ᵗʰ Infantry Division G3 Staff, "The 75ᵗʰ Infantry Division in Combat", Camp Baltimore, France, 1944, pages 26-28.

87. Google map of Dorsten, Germany, Google 2011.

88. 75ᵗʰ Infantry Division G3 Staff, "The 75ᵗʰ Infantry Division in Combat", Camp Baltimore, France, 1944, page 30.

89. Stegen, Bob, Phone conversation with Scott Adams, August 1, 2011.

90. Stegen, Bob, Phone conversation with Scott Adams, August 1, 2011.

91. 291ˢᵗ Infantry Regiment Staff, Overlay dated 31 March 1945, "Actions against the enemy report for February 1945", 291ˢᵗ Infantry Regiment, dated 2 March 1945.

92. Stegen, Bob, Phone conversation with Scott Adams, August 1, 2011.

93. "Battle of Okinawa", Wikipedia, http://en.wikipedia.org/wiki/Battle_of_okinawa, 2011.

94. Google map of Castrop-Rauxel, Germany, Google 2011.

95. Reither, Fred, "Written memories of World War 2", dated 26 January 1945

96. Carr, Larry, Email to Scott Adams, dated January 23,2012.

97. 291st Infantry Regiment Staff, Narrative, pages1-2, "Actions against the enemy report for April 1945", 291st Infantry Regiment, dated 2 May 1945.

98. Google map of Castrop-Rauxel, Germany, Google 2011.

99. Neville, Ed Written memories of World War2, undated, page 1.

100. Hayes, Bill, Written memories of World War 2, dated 20 May 1991.pages 3-4.

101. Stegen, Bob, Phone conversation with Scott Adams, August 1, 2011

102. Cox, Edgar, "Members of F Company killed and wounded in action during World War 2, page 3.

103. Stoddard, Ray, Written memories of World War 2 after Colmar Pocket, undated, pages 2-3

104. Huston, James, Biography of a Battalion, Stackpole Books, Mechanicsburg, PA, 2003, page 15.

105. Google map of Persbeck, Germany, Google 2011.

106. Henn, Nathan, Written memories of World War 2, undated, page 2.

107. Wuebben, Linda, "Crofton man 'finally' receives Bronze Star, news paper unknown, date unknown, pages unknown.

108. Stegen, Bob, Phone conversation with Scott Adams, August 1, 2011.

109. Google map of Persbeck, Germany, Google 2011.

110. 291st Infantry Regiment Staff, Narrative page 6, "Actions against the enemy report for April 1945", 291st Infantry Regiment, dated 2 May 1945.

111. "Walter Model", Wikipedia, enwikipedia.org/wiki/Walter_Model. Stoddard, Ray, email to Scott Adams, dated November 19, 2011.

112. Stoddard, Ray email to Scott Adams, dated November 19, 2001

113. Siakel, Dick, Phone conversation with Scott Adams, August 1, 2011.

114. "The Mule, 75th Infantry Division newspaper. May 18, 1945, page 3.

115. Siakel, Dick, Phone conversation with Scott Adams, August 1, 2011

116. www.104Infdiv.org/TRIBUTE.htm, General Omar Bradley's tribute to the rifleman.

117. Letourneau, Ed, TV 6 Greenfield Leon Weeks interview on Ed's memories of World War 2, June 25, 2000.

118. Neville, Ed, Written Memories of World War 2, undated

119. Siakel, Dick, Phone conversation with Scott Adams, August 1, 2011.

120. "The Mule", The 75th Infantry Division newspaper, April 27,1945, page 1

121. DeBruyn, Richard, "Fearful Frosty, Freezing and Frigid Flashbacks", The Guidon, undated, page 2.

122. "Atom Won War, Says Churchill" The Stars and Stripes, Volume 1 Number 82, August 16, 1945, page 1.

123. "75th Association Drive Launched", The Mule, The 75th Infantry Division newspaper, Volume 2 number 7, September 21, 1945, pages 1-3.

124. The Bulge Buster, Volume 1 number 1, May 1946 page 1.

125. "History of Division Broadcast to ETO", The Mule, The 75th Infantry Division newspaper, volume 2 number 7 September 21, 1945, page 2

126. "75th Gridmen in Scrimmage with AAC11" The Mule, The 75th Infantry Division newspaper, volume 2 number 7 September 21, 1945, pages 3-4.

127. Alexander, Larry, "The Biggest Brother, The life of Major Dick Winters, The Man who led the band of Brothers, New York, NAL Caliber, 2005, page 214.

128. Letourneau, Ed, TV 6 Greenfield Leon Weeks interview on Ed's memories of World War 2, June 25, 2000.

129. Stoddard, Ray, Email to Scott Adams, dated October 27, 2011.

130. Mule Cartoon, The Mule, Newspaper of 75th Infantry Division Volume Number 7, September 21, 1945, page 1.

131. Stoddard, Ray, Letter to Scott Adams, dated November 2, 2011

132. Huston, James, Biography of a Battalion, Stackpole Books, Mechanicsburg, PA, page 284.

133. Powers, Rod, "Bronze Star Medal", http://usmilitary.about.com/od/armymedals/ss/bsm_4.htm.

134. Wuebben, Linda, "Crofton man 'finally' receives Bronze Star, news paper unknown, date unknown, pages unknown.

135. Stoddard, Ray, Email to Scott Adams, dated November 19, 2011.

136. Honor Flight Network, www.honorflight.org.

137. Cox, Edgar, Lists of members of F Company killed and wounded in action during World War 2.

138. Coggins, David, The 75th Infantry Division, Turner Publishing Company, Kentucky, 1999, page 176.

139. Bowman, Paul, Clemson Alumni Association, http://cualumni.clemson.edu/page.aspx?pid=1453.

140. Stegen, Bob, Lists of Towns he was in during World War 2, undated, page 1.

141. 75th Infantry Division G3 staff, The 75th Infantry Division in Combat, Camp Baltimore, France, 1944, G3 map of Battle of Ardennes.

142. 75th Infantry Division G3 staff, The 75th Infantry Division in Combat, Camp Baltimore, France, 1944, G3 map of Colmar Pocket.

143. 75th Infantry Division G3 staff, The 75th Infantry Division in Combat, Camp Baltimore, France, 1944, G3 map of Battle for the Ruhr

INDEX

★ ★ ★

N

Neuf Brisach 49, 57

P

Persebeck 96, 98, 100, 101, 169
Poteau ix, 23, 30, 31, 32, 33, 34, 40

R

Rhine River 52, 53, 54, 56, 62, 67,
    68, 69, 70, 71, 73, 74, 75, 77,
    79, 125
Rutgers Castle 87, 97, 169

S

75th Battle Command Training
    Division 133
Sickingmuhle 81, 82, 83, 85, 169
South Wales 11
SS Edmund B Alexander 11
Statue of Liberty 11, 131

W

Wolfgantzen 47, 51, 52, 53, 58